How to Be an Intelligent Muslim

Muddassir Khan

Published by Muddassir Khan, 2024.

Table of Contents

How to Be an Intelligent Muslim

Muddassir Khan

The Gift of Intelligence

The Supreme Blessing of Intelligence

It is widely recognized that among the greatest blessings bestowed upon humanity is intelligence. This faculty serves as the tool through which we gain knowledge of our Creator. It enables us to discern beneficial things, understand the outcomes of events, grasp the concealed, and gather the fruits of wisdom.

Diversity in Human Intelligence and Experience

People vary in their levels of intelligence as well as in their knowledge and experience. Inspired by this diversity, Shaykh Ibn Jawzi (Allah have mercy on him) decided to compile the stories of exceptionally intelligent individuals known for their strong insight and wisdom into a book titled "Kitab al-Azkiya" (The Book of the Clever).

Objectives of the Book

1. Recognizing and Appreciating Intelligence

By recounting these stories, he aimed to introduce such individuals and acknowledge their value.

2. Inspiring Potentially Intelligent Minds

Another goal was to broaden the horizons of those who show a capacity to reach similar heights of wisdom. As Sharif al-Razi said, "I see with my eyes, and it is hoped that I will also hear with my ears." Engaging with the wise and observing their actions is beneficial. Listening to someone's story can be as enlightening as meeting them in person. It is reported that al-Ma'mun said, "There is nothing more beautiful than looking at intelligent people."

3. Correcting Self-Satisfied Minds

Finally, by narrating the stories of those whose intelligence cannot be matched, Ibn Jawzi's hope was to educate and correct those who are overly satisfied with their own views.

Success is Granted by Allah

Ultimately, success comes from Allah.

The Virtue of Intelligence

Wisdom from Prophet Muhammad (peace and blessings of Allah be upon him)

Ibn Abbas (Allah be pleased with him) once visited Aisha (may Allah be pleased with her) and asked, "O Mother of the Believers! One man prays little at night and sleeps a lot; another prays a lot and sleeps little. Which one is more virtuous?" Aisha replied, "I asked the Prophet (peace be upon him) the same question, and he said, 'The best of them are the most intelligent.' When I clarified that I was asking about their worship, he responded, 'O Aisha! People will be judged based on their intelligence. The more intelligent one is, the higher they will stand in both this world and the hereafter.'"

Advice from the Prophet Muhammad

According to a narration from Ibn Umar, Prophet Muhammad (peace be upon him) advised, "Do not admire someone's Islam until you understand the soundness of their intellect."

This Hadith highlights the importance of assessing a person's understanding and intelligence rather than merely their outward expressions of faith.

The Creation of Intelligence

Prophet Muhammad (peace be upon him) said: "Allah first created the pen, then the ink. He commanded the pen to write, and when it asked, 'What should I write?' Allah said, 'Write everything that has happened and will happen until the Day of Judgment.' Then, Allah created the intellect and declared, 'By My glory, I will perfect you in those I love, and I will leave you incomplete in those I despise.'"

This narration underscores the primordial significance of the intellect in the divine plan and its pivotal role in human life.

Abdurrahman b. Sabit narrates from Ibn Abbas:

"When Allah Almighty created the intellect, He said to it, 'Go!' and it went. He then said, 'Come!' and it came. After that, He said, 'By My Glory, I have not created anything better than you. Through you, I will give and take, and through you, I will reward and punish.'"

The Challenge of Tempting the Believer

Idris narrates that Wahb b. Munabbih said:

"I have observed from what Allah has revealed through His prophets: Satan struggles against nothing as much as he struggles against a believer. He can easily dominate a hundred ignorant people, using his tricks to subdue them all. But when he confronts a believer, no matter how much he tries, he cannot harm him even as much as plucking a single hair from his eyebrow. It is easier for Satan to uproot mountains stone by stone than to deceive an intelligent and discerning believer. For such a believer is more steadfast than a mountain and tougher than iron. Satan tries every trick to deceive him but fails. Frustrated, he exclaims to himself, 'Woe unto me! Why can't I overcome him?' Then, he turns away from the believer and focuses on the ignorant, whom he easily deceives into committing vile acts that bring worldly punishments like flogging, stoning, shaving of the head, hand-cutting, and hanging. Two people may appear equal in righteous deeds, but if one is more intelligent than the other, the difference between them can be as vast as the distance between the East and the West."

The Advice of Luqman (peace be upon him) to His Son

It is narrated that Luqman (peace be upon him) said to his son:

"My son! Be wise in your relationship with Allah! Among people, the most intelligent is the one whose deeds are the best. Satan flees from an intelligent person and cannot deceive him. O my son! No one has worshipped Allah with anything superior to intellect (reason)."

The Value of Intellect in Worship

Abu Al-Ala narrates from Mutrif:

"Mutrif said, 'After faith, no gift is superior to the intellect.'"

The Role of Intellect in the Hereafter

Huleyd b. Dalej narrates from Mu'awiya b. Qurrah:

"People perform Hajj, Umrah, engage in Jihad, pray, and fast; but on the Day of Judgment, they will be rewarded according to their intellect (level of understanding)."

Enjoying Paradise Proportionate to Intellect

It is narrated that Abu Zakariya said:

"A person in Paradise will enjoy according to his intellect."

Understanding the Nature and Place of the Intellect

Perspectives on the Nature of Intellect

Ahmad b. Hanbal's View on Intellect

Ahmad b. Hanbal said, "Intellect (the mind) is instinct."

Muhasibi's Description of Intellect

Muhasibi stated, "It is light."

Others' Opinions on Intellect

Some say, "Intellect is the power that allows us to discern the truth of knowledge," while others describe it as, "A type of necessary knowledge that shows the possibility of possible things and the impossibility of impossible things." There are those who describe it as "a simple essence" or "a transparent substance."

A Bedouin's Definition of Intellect

When asked, "What is intellect?" a Bedouin replied, "It is the essence you acquire through experience."

Four Meanings of Intellect

1. Distinguishing Humans from Animals

Intellect refers to the quality that distinguishes humans from animals, enabling humans to receive theoretical knowledge and to be prepared to learn complex arts that require contemplation. This is what is meant by the phrase "Intellect is instinct." It acts as a light reflecting on the heart, preparing a person to perceive things.

2. Knowledge of Possibilities

Intellect is the knowledge placed within human nature that allows one to discern what is possible from what is not.

3. Knowledge Gained from Experience

Intellect is also the knowledge gained through benefiting from experiences and is referred to as wisdom.

4. Mastery Over Desires

Intellect is the pinnacle of the natural power by which we suppress the desires that invite us to fleeting pleasures and delights.

The Etymology of "Intellect"

Sa'leb's Explanation

Sa'leb explains the root of the word "intellect" as coming from the concept of restraint. For example, "Aqal-tu'n-naqa" means "I restrained the camel from moving." Similarly, the phrase "Aqala batn'ur-ree'u" is used to describe someone who is constipated.

The Location of Intellect

Views on the Physical Seat of Intellect

Fadl b. Ziyad narrates that Ahmad b. Hanbal (Allah have mercy on him) believed the seat of intellect is in the brain, a view shared by Abu Hanifa (Allah have mercy on him). However, some scholars from our tradition, including Imam Shafi'I (Allah have mercy on him), argue that intellect resides in the heart.

Quranic Evidence Supporting the Heart

Those who support the heart as the seat of intellect cite Quranic verses such as, "If they had traveled through the earth, they would have hearts with which to understand" (Hajj 22:46), and, "Indeed, in this is a reminder for those who have a heart" (Qaf 50:37), suggesting that the heart is the center of intellect.

Understanding Mind, Comprehension, and Intelligence

The Essence of Intelligence

As understood from the Ibn Jawzi's explanations, the term "intelligence" refers to the state of something reaching completion and perfection. True intelligence is the capacity to quickly and thoroughly understand and grasp the essence of spoken words or lived experiences. This ability also determines a person's level of intelligence.

Signs Indicating Intelligence and Wisdom

Limit of the Mind

The limit of the mind is its capacity to receive thoughts and ideas.

Boundaries of Understanding

The boundary of understanding is having good preparation for this capacity.

Upper Limit of Intelligence

The upper limit of intelligence is the ability to use this capacity quickly and efficiently. A person of intellect understands the meaning as soon as they hear a word.

Different Perspectives on Intelligence

Some have said, "The upper limit of intelligence is the power of comprehension; lack of understanding is weakness." Zeccaac also commented, "Intelligence is like the complete expression in language. Aging indicates superior understanding. Superior understanding means being quick and sufficient."

Aboo Bakir b. Anboori's Perspective

Aboo Bakir b. Anboori said, "So-and-so is intelligent," meaning their insight and alertness are complete.

Signs Pointing to Intelligence and Wisdom

Criteria Based on Appearance and Actions

Aclaa narrates, "One day while sitting at home, Ziyad entered and asked, 'Has an intelligent person visited you?' Not knowing whom he meant, I replied. 'An intelligent person is recognizable by their face and stature,' he said. Upon hearing this, I went outside and found someone with a beautiful face, tall stature, and eloquent speech. I invited him in, and Ziyad asked him for his opinion on a matter. The man replied, 'I am uncomfortable. A person in discomfort cannot form opinions,' indicating his need to use the restroom. Later, he said, 'I am hungry. The hungry have no opinions,' until I brought food. After eating, he said, 'Now you can ask me anything.' He showed knowledge in every question asked."

Speech and Actions Indicating Intelligence

The signs of an intelligent person include silence, composure, keeping their eyes guarded and moving appropriately, and observing the outcomes of events. They do not succumb to fleeting desires that lead to harm. They choose the best and purest in food, drink, clothing, words, and actions, avoiding things of uncertain consequences.

Abu'd-Derdaa's Perspective

Abu'd-Derdaa said, "Would you like me to tell you a sign of intelligence? An intelligent person shows humility to those above them and does not despise those beneath them. They do not speak in vain and treat people according to their character. They strengthen their faith in their Lord, continue their path in this world with caution and discretion."

Wahb b. Munebbih's Narration of Lukman's Advice

Wahb b. Munebbih narrates Lukman's advice to his son, "O my son! Intelligence is not complete without ten qualities: ensuring humility and potential for maturity, taking only what is necessary from the world and spending the surplus in charity, valuing humility more than honor and power. Never getting tired of seeking knowledge throughout life. Not underestimating one's needs. Appreciating the good deeds of others while belittling one's own. The tenth quality that elevates a person and ensures their good reputation is seeing everyone in the world as superior to oneself. Being joyful upon encountering someone better and wishing to reach their level. And if he sees someone worse than him, he says, "Perhaps this one will be saved and I will perish."

Usman b. Abdurrahman's Account from Mekhool

Usman b. Abdurrahman narrates from Mekhool that Lukman said, "The greatest honor and peace is achieved through complete intellect. Intelligence covers all sins, corrects mistakes and evils, making the Lord pleased with them."

Abaan b. Cerir's Narration from Muhelleb b. Safra

Abaan b. Cerir narrates Muhelleb b. Safra saying, "It pleases me when a wise person controls their tongue, but it displeases me when their tongue controls their wisdom."

Foolishness and Its Meaning

Ibnul-A'rabi says: The word "al-Hamaka" is derived from the phrase "the market was devastated," indicating that the mind and insight of the one considered foolish have been devastated, so he is not consulted in matters of war, and his opinion is not respected.

Abu Bakr al-Makarim states: "Pigweed are named foolish because they grow by the waterway and are burdened by camels."

Ibnul-A'rabi also states: "A person is called foolish for this reason. Because the seriousness of his speech cannot be distinguished from the non-serious, and the soft from the hard."

The difference between Foolishness and Madness

We have examined the word "fool" from the standpoint of language. Because it cannot reach the goal without understanding the meaning. Foolishness and negligence, unlike madness, follow the wrong path and use the wrong method even though the goal is correct. Because madness consists of defects in purpose and method. In short, a fool is one who follows the wrong path despite having a correct goal and acts wrongly while advancing towards achieving that goal.

The madman is the one whose primary starting point is wrong. A madman is one who chooses what should not be chosen. We (Ibn Jawzi) will explain this by giving examples of some distracted ones whose stories we will tell.

Here is an example: When a governor's bird escapes and he orders the city gates to be closed.

The governor's primary purpose was to prevent the bird from escaping.

Anatomy of Foolishness

Narrated by Abu Ishaq: "If you hear that a rich man has become poor, or a poor man has become rich, or that a living person has died, believe it. But if you hear that a fool has become wise, never believe it."

"There are three things: believe two of them and do not believe one. If someone tells you that someone who is with you turned his back on the wall and died, believe it. If a poor man goes to a country and becomes rich, believe it. But if someone tells you that a fool went to a country and became wise, do not believe it."

The Remedy for Foolishness

Awzai says: "I heard that they asked Jesus (peace be upon him): 'O Messenger of Allah, you revive the dead by the permission of Allah! You heal the congenitally blind by the permission of Allah! So what is the remedy for foolishness?' He said, 'That indeed has left me helpless.'"

Ja'far ibn Muhammad said: "In the view of a fool, manners are like water flowing into the bottom of a melon. As water is absorbed, the melon becomes bitter."

Foolishness is Worse than Being Mistaken

Ma'mun tells: "Do you know what happened between me and Harun al-Rashid, the leader of Muslims? I made a mistake. When I went up to him and greeted him, he said to me, 'Get lost, you fool!' I got angry and left. I did not go near him for a while. He sent me the following verses on a piece of paper:

If only my words were different; the separation has become long. Is the mistake in you or in me? If you have wronged us, may Allah forgive you. If I have wronged you, then forgive me.

Upon this, I went to him. 'If the mistake is mine, we seek forgiveness. If it is yours, we have forgiven it,' he said. I said, 'You called me a fool; if you had said I was mistaken, it would have been lighter.' Foolishness is anatomical. Some poets have said, 'When bodies are sick, treating them is easier than treating the mind.'"

People Differ in Foolishness

Foolishness is the Lack of Sound Judgment

Foolishness is defined as the absence of sound judgment. As previously stated, foolishness results from the mind or intellect not being healthy. It is not possible to correct or punish something that is inherent from creation. However, it is possible to educate and correct someone who is fundamentally sound but has shortcomings. In short, people differ in their intellect, and therefore, they also differ in foolishness.

When asked about the limit of foolishness, Ibrahim en-Nazzam replied, "You are asking about the limit of something that has no limit."

When Umar (Allah be pleased with him) read the verse:

"O, Man! What has misled you concerning your generous Lord?" (Surah al-Infitar 82:6)

He said, "O my Lord! Folly (Foolishness)!"

Ali (Allah be pleased with him) said, "There is some type of foolishness in every person, and they live with it."

Wahb Ibn Munabbih said, "Allah has created humans to be foolish (in one aspect). If not, they would not be happy in life."

Mutarrif mentioned, "I hope to keep my promise. There is no one who is not foolish in their dealings with Allah. However, some people's foolishness is lighter than others."

Sufyan al-Thawri said, "Humans were created to live, and they have to be foolish to live."

Some poets said,

"Indeed, those who escape do so not because of their deficiency but because of the deficiency of their intelligence."

The Characteristics of Fools

Moral Characteristics of Fools

The second part of foolishness pertains to individuals' behavior and actions. Not taking heed from the consequences of events, relying on the unknown, and lack of affection are examples of such behaviors.

Self-Admiration and Excessive Talk

Abu'd-Darda said, "Even if a person has elegance and speaks properly, and even if he prays at night and fasts during the day, do not be deceived by these three traits: self-admiration, excessive talk on irrelevant matters, and feeling superior for doing something himself but belittling others for the same. These are signs of ignorance."

Umar ibn Abdulaziz (Allah be pleased with him) said: "Two habits of a fool never disappear: responding quickly and looking around excessively."

One man talked a lot in front of Muawiyah. When Muawiyah said, "Be quiet!", the man replied, "Did I even talk?"

Ignorance

One of the attributes of a fool is ignorance. Because even a little bit of intellect allows a person to learn something. If a person has not learned anything despite advancing in age, it indicates that he is a fool.

Al-Amash said: "Whenever I see an old man who knows nothing, I feel like slapping him."

Abdullah ibn Muawiyah was a friend of Al-Walid. He would come to him, and they would converse. One day, they started playing a game. Meanwhile, an attendant came and said, 'May Allah bless the ruler! Your uncle from the nobles of Thakif wishes to visit you.' Walid said, 'Let him go (ignore him).' Abdullah said, 'What harm would it do if you let him come? Let our game remain as it is. After meeting with the man, we will continue our game,' said Abdullah. Walid accepted Abdullah's proposal and said, 'Let him in.' He came in, looking dignified with marks of prostration on his forehead, wearing a turban, and neatly trimmed beard! He greeted them and said, 'May Allah bless the ruler! I have come as a veteran to visit you and fulfill my rights.' Their conversation continued as follows:

- Welcome! May Allah bless you. (After a short pause)

- My dear uncle, have you memorized the Quran?

- No! I couldn't memorize due to being busy.

- Did you learn something from the sayings and life of the Prophet (peace be upon him)?

- No!

- Do you know the stories and poems of the Arabs?

- No!

- Do you know the stories and literature of non-Arabs?

- I didn't seek that!

After hearing his responses they came to know that there is no benefit in talking to him further and continued playing the game.

A Fool Likes False Praise

One of the characteristics of a fool is liking false praise and respect, even if undeserved.

Al-Asma'i said: "If you want to understand if someone is intelligent, tell an untrue story during a conversation. If you see him listening and accepting it, he is a fool. If he does not accept it, he is intelligent."

Some scholars have said: "Among the qualities of foolish people are the following: Hastiness, frivolity, hard-heartedness, pride, sinfulness, ignorance, simple-mindedness, sluggishness, treachery, oppression, compromise, heedlessness, rejoicing in others' misfortunes, arrogance, deceitfulness, considering oneself insignificant when not in need, losing hope when in need, overreacting to joy, speaking ill when speaking, being stingy when asked for something, insisting when desiring something, not understanding what is said, laughing loudly, and collapsing when crying."

A Fool is Recognized by Six Traits

Some scholars have said: "A fool is recognized by six traits: Getting angry without reason, giving charity in inappropriate places, speaking without benefit, trusting everyone, inability to keep secrets, inability to distinguish between friend and foe, speaking whatever comes to mind, and thinking oneself the wisest among people."

Signs of Foolishness

Abu Hatim ibn Hayyan al-Hafiz said: "The signs of foolishness are: Responding hastily, abandoning certainty, laughing excessively, looking around excessively, speaking ill of honorable people, and associating with wicked people. A fool is one who, when you turn away from him, seeks an opportunity; when you draw near to him, ignores you; when you withhold your help, denies your right; when you deny his right, displays knowledge; when you do good, returns evil; when you do evil, shows kindness; when you oppress, seeks justice; and when he oppresses you, expects no justice. If you are in the company of a fool, be grateful to Allah for the intellect given to you and not to him."

Dangers of Being Friends with Fools

Ibn Abi Ziyad narrated: My father said to me, "O my son! Keep the company of intelligent people, interact with them, and beware of the fool! For whenever I sit with a fool, I feel my intellect diminishing."

Do Not Get Angry at Fools!

It is narrated from Abdullah ibn Habib: "Allah (the Most High) revealed to Moses (peace be upon him), 'Do not get angry with fools, lest your pain increases.'"

Hasan al-Basri said: "Deserting a fool is a sign of closeness to Allah."

Salman ibn Musa narrated: "It is impossible for three things to be found together: Understanding in a fool, nobility in an ignorant person, and goodness in a wrongdoer."

People are of Four Types

Halil ibn Ahmed reported from Ahmad ibn Qays: "People are of four types: The one who knows and knows that he knows; he is a scholar, so seek benefit from him. The one who knows but does not know that he knows; he is an ordinary person, so teach him. The one who does not know but knows that he does not know; he is a seeker of knowledge, so give him knowledge. The one who does not know and does not know that he does not know; he is a fool, so reject him."

People are of four types. Speak only with three of them: Speak with the one who knows (both the one who is aware and the one who is not aware that he knows) and the one who acknowledges his ignorance. Do not speak with the one who does not know but thinks he knows."

Ja'far ibn Muhammad said: "People are of four types: The one who knows and knows that he knows; learn from him. The one who knows but is unaware of what he knows; he is asleep, so wake him up. The one who does not know but is aware of his ignorance; he is ignorant, so educate him. The one who does not know and is unaware of his ignorance; he is a fool, so beware of him."

Amash said: "To rebuke a fool is like blowing air into a wool sack."

An Unintelligent Friend is More Dangerous

It is narrated from Abdullah b. Hureybi: "Every unintelligent friend is more of an enemy to you than your actual enemies."

It is narrated from Bishr b. Harith: "Looking at a fool burns the eyes. There will come a time when fools will gain power."

Avoid Sitting with Fools!

It is narrated from Shu'ba: "Our intellect is already deficient! When we sit and converse with someone even less intelligent, our own deficiency becomes more pronounced. I believe that sitting with someone less intelligent than oneself causes harm."

Some scholars have said: "The burden of the intelligent falls on themselves. The burden (distress) of the fool falls on others. For the unintelligent, there is neither this world nor the Hereafter."

How to Deal with a Fool

One of the scholars said: "Everyone does not know how to deal with a fool, and I am the one who knows this best." When asked how to deal with them, he said, "Give them less than what they deserve (that is less that their due), so that they ask for more. Because even when you give them their due, they still want more."

Some poets have said: "Beware of befriending a fool! A fool is like a torn garment. When you mend one part, the wind tears another weak part. Or like a shattered glass that, when broken, will not mend, or like a child in the market who, when fed, bites people; when hungry, he cries, and when scolded, he corrupts the gathering with his foolishness!"

Arabs known for their foolishness and metaphors about them

The Arabs sometimes make metaphors about those known for their foolishness, sometimes comparing them to various animals and birds, or imagining foolish behavior even if it hasn't occurred.

Fools Who Are Compared

The Arabs say: "More foolish than Habnaka." "More foolish than Hazane."

The Arabs say: "More foolish than Abu Gabshan, more foolish than Juha, more foolish than Ajel Lujaym, more foolish than Hujayna, more foolish than Beyhes, more foolish than Malik b. Zeyd-i Menat, more foolish than Adiy b. Habbab and Mahmure!"

Tales of those known for their foolishness and absence of mind

Foolish Hebneka

His name is Yezid b. Shervan. He is also called Ibn Mervan. He is from the tribe of Kays b. Salebe. One of the foolish behaviors he displayed is as follows: One day he put a ring made of beads, bones, and ceramic pieces around his neck. "I fear losing myself, and I did this to know myself!" he said. One night, the ring came off his neck and fell onto his brother's neck. When he woke up, he said to his brother, "You are me, so who am I?"

Hebneka once lost his camel and shouted, "Whoever finds the camel owns it." He was asked "so why search for it." He told, "For the pleasure of finding it!".

According to another account, he said, "Whoever finds the camel shall have ten camels," and asked, "Why are you doing this?" When asked, he said, "Finding the lost gives pleasure to the heart."

The tribes of Tafawa and the Rasipogullar, argued about a man and which tribe he belongs to. Hebneka said, "Let's throw him into the water; if he sinks, he is from the Rasipogullar. If not, he is from the Tafawe!" Upon this, the man said, "If this is the judgment, then I abstain from both tribes."

Hebneka grazed the sheep and he would give food to the fat sheep and keep it away from the skinny ones, saying, "I cannot fix what Allah has broken."

One of the fools, Abu Gabsan, lived near the Kaaba and gathered in Taif to drink with Kusay b. Kilab. When Gabsan got drunk, Kusay purchased the keys (the guardianship) of the Kaaba from him with a sack of wine. He then took the keys, went to Makkah, and said, "O Quraysh! These keys are for the Kaaba made by your father Ismail. Allah returned them without oppression or treachery," Abu Gabsan was very sorry. After this, among the Arabs, "More sorry than Abu Gabsan, more in trouble than Abu Gabsan, and more foolish than Abu Gabsan..." started to be said.

Acel b. Luceym b. Sa'b b. Ali b. Bakir b. Wail. It was said to him, "What did you name your horse?" Upon this, he stood up, gouged out one eye of the horse, and said, "I named him Blind!"

Muhammad b. Alaa al-Kaatib narrates: "Hamza b. Beyz had a servant. He asked his servant, "Which day did you perform Friday prayer in Rusafa?" After a moment's hesitation, the servant replied, "Tuesday!"

Juha

One day, Juha visited a friend of his and found him sick, suffering from stomach pain. Juha hurried to bring a doctor for him.

When the doctor entered the room of Juha's sick friend, he said to him, 'Open your mouth.' He looked inside for a while, then glanced at the ground, thought for a moment, and said, 'You have eaten a lot of cakes. Don't do that again.'"

Juha was surprised by the doctor's quick diagnosis of the illness, so he asked him, 'But how did you know that so quickly?' The doctor replied, 'It's simple. When I learned that he was suffering from stomach pains, I began to look for the cause. I looked inside his mouth and saw food remnants resembling cake. Then I looked at the ground and saw cake crumbs scattered around. That confirmed to me that he had indulged excessively in eating cakes, which are heavy with fats that burden the stomach.'"

So Juha said, 'The view of a wise man and a prophetic doctor.' After sitting with his friend for a while to comfort him, Juha returned home believing that the profession of medicine depends not only on intelligence but also on keen observation. And here he had gained and learned an important lesson.

After a few days, while Juha was riding his donkey on the road, he met a friend whom he hadn't seen in a long time. Juha greeted him with great joy, dismounted from his donkey, and warmly kissed his friend and greeted him affectionately. Juha noticed that his friend was sad and troubled, so he asked him about the reason for all this sadness. The friend replied in a sorrowful voice, 'My father is ill, and I am now on my way to fetch the doctor for him.'

Juha shouted loudly, "Why call a doctor when I am here, my friend??"

"Did you not know that I treat the sick?" Juha exclaimed, pushing his friend. The friend tried to stop him and pleaded for him to cease his joking. But Juha insisted, saying, "Don't worry... the cure for your father is with me..."

When they arrived at the house, Juha examined the patient's mouth for a moment, then sighed. He looked around the floor and under the bed. He nodded his head like an expert scholar, then returned to look under the bed. The father had his shoes stored under the bed. Juha whispered to his friend, "Don't worry, my friend, it's a simple matter. We've learned from books and wise men that the habit of eating shoes is bad and harmful to health. So, I advise you to keep the shoes away from under your father's bed to ensure he completely stops the habit of eating shoes." The friend was so astonished that he fell to the floor, fainting in disbelief.

Once Juha went to the market looking for a strong donkey. He bought the donkey and tied it with a strong rope, then walked, dragging it behind him.

There were two cunning thieves watching Juha. Along the way, one of the thieves approached, untied the rope, and placed it around his own neck while the other thief took the donkey. After a while, Juha looked back and was struck with great astonishment. He was speechless upon finding a man of flesh and blood, with a mustache and a beard, tied to the rope.

Juha thought for a moment, then asked him, "Where is my donkey? What have you done with it? Speak, or I will take you to the chief of police."

The man, trembling and showing fear and panic, stammered, "I... I, sir, was the donkey..."

Juha, puzzled, replied, "Are you lying to me? How can this be?"

The con man explained, "I was once a young and reckless boy, disobedient to my mother. I didn't listen to her or bring her what she asked for. One day, she was sick and asked me to fetch a doctor, but I was very lazy and a useless boy. I told her, 'I'm sleepy and I want to sleep.' Her condition worsened during the night, and in her severe pain, she raised her hands to the sky and prayed for God to turn me into a donkey.

Today, my mother forgave me. If I had a lot of money, I would give it to you, but I don't have any money at all..."

Juha, standing there, listened to the man, astonished and bewildered, then said, "There is no power and no strength except with Allah. Glory be to Allah. I ask for Allah's forgiveness. How could I have used you while you were a human being... God forbid... Go, my boy, go to your mother and seek her forgiveness, and never anger her again."

Juha then went home and told his wife about this strange incident. The next morning, Juha went back to the market to buy another new donkey. He was shocked and stood frozen, unable to move...

He saw the donkey he had bought yesterday standing among a group of donkeys.

He asked the seller about this donkey. The seller replied, "An old woman came early this morning and sold me the donkey..."

One of the thieves had disguised himself as an old woman and sold the donkey to the trader, and then they shared the money between them.

Juha approached the donkey and put his mouth to its ear and said, while the trader watched in utter amazement, "Oh, you wretch... You returned to disobeying your mother... Didn't I tell you not to anger her? Didn't you learn from your harsh experience?? You truly deserve what has happened to you...

By God, I will never buy you again so that you don't do the same to me as you did last time. You do not deserve kindness or forgiveness. I will leave you here with the donkeys as a punishment for your disobedience to your mother. And perhaps a new trader will buy you to carry tons of burdens on your back, which you deserve for your bad actions..."

Once Juha went to the market as usual to spend his time indulging in his favorite hobby: wandering through the market and searching for different new goods.

The people in the market were often annoyed by Juha and his numerous questions about the merchandise, despite his habit of not buying anything.

There was a man who wanted to teach Juha a lesson and make him the laughingstock of the market. He made a bet with some of the merchants that he could slap Juha on the face without Juha being able to take him to court. The merchants were amused by the idea.

The man stood waiting for Juha to pass by. When Juha approached a shop to examine a product and turned his back to the road and faced the shop, the man came up from behind and slapped Juha hard on the cheek. Juha staggered and almost fell to the ground.

Juha managed to regain his composure, turned around, and was about to fight the man.

However, the man quickly apologized, saying, "I'm sorry, Juha. I mistook you for another man who stole from me some time ago."

Juha didn't accept the excuse and lunged at the man to seek retribution. The merchants intervened, saying to Juha, "The man is right." They even testified to this.

Juha sensed there was some sort of trick.

He said to them, "I won't be satisfied until we go to court..."

They replied, "Choose one of our senior merchants to judge between you." Juha chose one of the merchants, who was one of the most irritated by Juha.

The merchant came forward and listened to Juha's complaint, pretending he knew nothing about the slap.

The merchant asked the man, "Why did you slap Juha so hard?"

The man replied, "Forgive me, sir, I thought he was a thief..."

The merchant asked, "Did you apologize to him?"

The man said, "Yes, I did."

The merchant then turned to Juha and said, "Juha, do you accept his apology?"

Juha refused, demanding compensation to restore his honor.

At this point, the merchant asked, "Do you both agree to my judgment?"

Juha and the man both agreed, and all the merchants in the market witnessed it.

The merchant then said to the man, "You must pay Juha a fine of 20 dinars for slapping him."

The man protested, "But sir, I don't have that amount of money with me right now."

The merchant, winking at the man said, "Juha, can you give him a loan of 20 dinars so that he can pay you."

Juha readily agreed to do this and was happy that justice was served.

One day, Juha was alone in his house after his wife had gone to visit her sister in a nearby town. She had told him that she would spend the night there and return the next day.

That night, Juha felt lost, sad, and troubled because he was alone in the house while his wife was away.

He turned off all the lights in the house and went to bed early.

There was a thief who was observing the house. He noticed the lights were off early in the night, so he thought that everyone in the house might not be there. Especially since he had seen Juha's wife leaving the house in the morning with a bag full of her belongings.

The thief became excited, thinking it was an opportune moment to break into Juha's house, believing it was full of money and jewels.

Quietly, the thief entered the house. However, Juha had not yet fallen asleep.

Juha came to know that a thief had entered his house and therefore hid in a small box in his room and curled up inside it easily due to its small size.

The thief began searching here and there for a supposed treasure, but he found nothing.

Then he looked for something of lesser value to steal, but he couldn't find anything worth taking.

After a long search, he noticed the box in the corner of the room, which he hadn't noticed before. He thought to himself, "Perhaps there's something valuable in it."

The thief opened the box and was surprised to find Juha curled up inside.

Startled by the unexpected sight, the thief recoiled and shouted, "What are you doing here, Juha?"

Juha calmly replied, "Don't blame me, sir. I knew you wouldn't find anything to steal, so I felt ashamed of you and hid inside this box."

A man said to Juha: "I heard shouting from your house?" Juha replied, "My shirt fell down!" The man asked, "What happens if a shirt falls?" Juha retorted, "Oh fool! If you were inside the shirt, wouldn't you fall with it?"

Once Juha was troubled by the wind and said, "No one understands you but Solomon, son of David!"

One day, Juha burned incense, and his clothes caught fire. He exclaimed, "By Allah, the next time I burn incense, I will do it naked!"

A violent storm arose one day, and people started praying to Allah and repenting (which was the correct and appropriate response). Juha said, "O people! Don't rush to repent; the storm will soon pass!"

Due to demolition and other reasons, soil accumulated at the door of Juha's house. His father said, "The neighbors are pushing me to remove the soil. I need help. I need someone to make bricks. I don't know what to do. Tell me! What would you do if you were me?"

Juha said, "I would dig a hole and bury the accumulated soil!"

It is told that Juha once buried a few gold coins in the desert and marked the spot by the cloud overhead.

When Juha's father passed away, people told him, "Go and buy a shroud." Juha replied, "I'm afraid I'll miss the funeral prayer if I go to buy the shroud!"

Caliph Mehdi, wanting to joke around, summoned Juha. He had the skin used for executions spread on the ground and a sword placed on it. He pretended to execute Juha. When Juha sat down for the execution, he said to the executioner, "Be careful! Don't touch the spots where I had cupping done. I've just been cupped!"

One day, Juha entered the Friday mosque and asked, "What is this place?" They told him, "This is the Friday mosque." He then said, "May Allah have mercy on Friday! What a beautiful mosque it has built!"

One day, Juha walked by a group of people with peaches in his apron. He said, "If anyone can guess what I'm carrying in my apron, I'll give them the biggest peach!"

Once, Juha's father was preparing to go to Makkah for the pilgrimage (Hajj). Juha said to him, "For God's sake, don't stay too long! Try to be back in time for the festival of sacrifice!"

Stories of Intelligent People Who Committed Acts of Foolishness

A Worshipper and Leader Among Angels

Iblis, once a respected worshipper and leader among the angels, fell into foolishness and idiocy, surpassing even the most foolish.

Envy and Defiance at Adam's Creation

Upon witnessing Adam (peace be upon him) being created from clay, he pondered, "If I was preferred over him, I will destroy him, and if he was preferred over me, I will disobey him."

Ignorance of Divine Decree

Had he reflected, he would have realized Adam was chosen, and his envy should have ceased. Instead, he challenged Allah's decision, asking,

"Do You see this one whom You have honoured above me?" [al-Isra' 17: 62]

and claiming superiority over Adam ('alayhi as-salam) by stating,

"You created me from fire and created him from clay." [al-A'raf 7: 12].

Arrogance and False Superiority

His words implied, "I am wiser than the Most Wise (al-Hakim) and more knowledgeable than the All-Knowing (al-'Alim), and Your preference of Adam was incorrect."

The Path to Destruction

When his arguments failed, Iblis resolved to destroy himself and persisted in his stubbornness. He vowed,

"I will surely mislead them." [Sad 38: 82]

Ignorance in Defiance

His ignorance in this statement is twofold: Firstly, he aimed to challenge Allah, unaware that Allah is beyond influence or harm, being self-sufficient and absolute in truth.

Secondly, he forgot that he cannot mislead those whom Allah protects, but then he remembered and said, "Except Your chosen servants among them." [al-Hijr 15: 40]

Frustration in Futility

His actions proved ineffective, unable to sway those guided by Allah. His knowledge thus became futile.

Temporary Respite and Weak Resolve

Due to his weak resolve, he sought a short reprieve, knowing it would pass swiftly, when he requested, "Grant me reprieve until the Day they are resurrected." [al-A'raf 7: 14]

Misguided Delight in Sin

He finds pleasure in leading sinners astray, ignorantly thinking he can provoke Allah, forgetting the impending eternal punishment.

The Ultimate Ignorance

He overlooks the imminent punishment, displaying unparalleled idiocy and ignorance.

Astonishing Arrogance

Reflecting on Iblis's arrogance and malicious intent, that he refused to bow to Adam and instead became a tempter of his descendants.

Extreme Foolishness in Abu'l-Husayn al-Rawindi

Comparing to Iblis, Abu'l-Husayn al-Rawindi stands out in madness and idiocy, insulting the Prophets ('alayhum as-salām) and challenging the Qur'an with baseless accusations.

Blasphemous Claims

He dared to attribute injustice and evil to Allah, using derogatory language that defies the Creator's exaltedness.

Allah remains exalted above the folly of those who dare to argue against Him, showcasing His perfect wisdom and attributes.

Some Actions of Foolishness

The Foolishness of Qabil (Cain)

Among the tales of foolishness is that of Qabil (Cain). Following Iblis's footsteps in idiocy, Qabil displayed great foolishness when he threatened his brother by saying, "I will surely kill you" [al-Ma'idah 5: 27]. This threat was profoundly foolish, as he should have reflected on why his brother's sacrifice was accepted while his own was not. His idiocy further manifested when he carried his brother's body on his back, unable to figure out how to bury it.

The Folly of Idol Worshippers

Consider the idiocy of those who, in defense of their gods, declared, "Burn him and support your gods if you are to act." [al-Anbiya' 21: 68] and "Continue, and be patient over [the defense of your Gods]." [Sad 38: 6]. These words, mentioned in the Qur'an, highlight the extreme foolishness of those who would go to such lengths to support their false deities.

The Ignorance of King Nimrod

Another example of sheer idiocy is King Nimrod, who contended with Prophet Ibrāhīm ('alayhi as-salām) by arrogantly proclaiming, "I give life and cause death." [al-Baqarah 2: 258]. This declaration reflects his delusional belief in his own divine powers.

The Delusions of Pharaoh

Among the most glaring examples of foolishness is that of Pharaoh of Egypt. He boastfully questioned, "Does not the kingdom of Egypt belong to me, and these rivers flowing beneath me?" [al-Zukhruf (43):

51]. He took pride in the Nile, a river whose flow he did not command, nor did he comprehend its source or end. He ignored the existence of many other rivers not under his control. Pharaoh's ultimate foolishness was his claim to divinity. A story exemplifying this is when Iblis visited Pharaoh. Upon being asked who he was, Iblis replied, "I am Iblis." Pharaoh inquired, "What brings you here?" Iblis responded, "I came to observe and marvel at your madness." When Pharaoh questioned him, Iblis explained, "I was cast out and cursed for defying a creature like myself, while you audaciously claim to be a deity. This is madness indeed."

The Absurdity of Idol Worship

Among the most astonishing acts of idiocy is the worship of idols. The true deity is the creator, not something created by human hands. Nimrod's idiocy extended to building a tower to shoot an arrow at the sky, aiming to kill the deity of the heavens.

The Brothers of Yusuf (Joseph) and Their Folly

The brothers of Yūsuf ('alayhi as-salām) also displayed idiocy when they claimed, "A wolf ate him" [Yūsuf 12: 17], yet his shirt remained untorn.

The Foolishness of the Israelites

Another bizarre instance of idiocy is seen in the Children of Israel who, after being saved by Prophet Moosa ('alayhi as-salaam) from the sea, asked him to "make for us a God" [al-A'raf 7:138]. This request came after witnessing divine miracles firsthand.

The Christian Delusion of Divinity

Equally foolish is the Christian claim that Prophet Eesa ('alayhi as-salām) is a God or the Son of God. They ascribe divinity to a man who did not exist before his birth and who needed food to sustain himself. The Divine is independent and not reliant on anything. Furthermore, they claim he is the son of Allah, suggesting that he is either a part of or equal to Allah, both concepts that are impossible regarding Allah. Their assertion that he was killed and crucified further portrays him as helpless and incapable of self-defense, revealing the depth of their delusional idiocy.

The Folly of the Rafidah's Beliefs

Misunderstanding Ali's Actions

The Rafidah exhibit another form of idiocy through their beliefs about 'Ali (radiy Allahu 'anhu). They acknowledge that 'Ali accepted the pledges of allegiance (bay'ah) to Abu Bakr (radiy Allahu 'anhu) and 'Umar (radiy Allahu 'anhu). 'Ali also had children with Al-Hanafiyah, who was a captive during Abū Bakr's rule, and he married his daughter Umm Kulthum to 'Umar Ibn Al-Khattab (radiy Allahu 'anhu). These actions clearly show his acceptance and support of their leadership.

Contradictory Accusations

Despite these facts, the Rafidah foolishly accuse Abū Bakr and 'Umar of blasphemy and insult them, claiming to love and support 'Ali. However, their actions and beliefs are contradictory to 'Ali's stance and prove that they have strayed far from their purported loyalty to him.

Briefly Highlighting Foolishness

A Broad Look at Foolish Actions

If we examine similar foolish beliefs and actions, we will find many more examples. We present them briefly here to provoke thought and reflection. We choose not to delve into extensive details, as the primary purpose of this book lies elsewhere.

The Statement of Ahmad Ibn Hanbal

A Man's Oath and Speaking to a Fool

It is narrated that Ahmad Ibn Hanbal once said, "If a man came to me and said, 'I have made an oath of divorce not to talk to a fool that day,' and then he spoke to a Rafidi or a Christian, I would say, 'He did break his oath.'" Al-Daynūrī, puzzled, asked, "Why are they considered fools?"

Explaining Their Foolishness

Ahmad replied, "They are fools because they contradict the teachings of those they claim to follow. For instance, [Prophet] 'Isā ('alayhi as-salám) told the Christians to 'Worship Allah' [al-Ma'idah 5: 117] and stated, 'Indeed, I am the servant of Allah' [Maryam 19: 30]. Yet, they insist that he is not a servant but is Allah Himself."

The Rafidah's Contradiction

Ahmad further explained that 'Ali (radiy Allahu 'anhu) narrated the Prophet's (peace and blessings of Allah be upon him) words praising Abū Bakr and 'Umar, saying, "These two are the masters of the elder people among the inhabitants of Paradise." Nevertheless, the Rafidah insult and renounce them, acting contrary to 'Ali's respect for these companions.

The Idiocy of Ancient Times

An Example from Ancient Times

Besides, one of the most astonishing stories of idiocy from ancient times is narrated by Jābir Ibn 'Abdullah (radiy Allahu 'anhuma). He told of a man who worshipped Allah in a monastery. One day, after it rained and grass grew, the man saw a donkey eating the grass. Foolishly, he said, "O Allah, if you had a donkey, I would have herded it to eat with my donkey."

When news of this reached a prophet from the Children of Israel, he considered praying against the man for his stupidity. However, Allah revealed to him, "I only take account of people in accordance with their intellect." This illustrates that divine judgment is based on the capacity of one's understanding, highlighting the varying degrees of foolishness among people.

Narrations Indicating the Intelligence of Past Prophets

Evidence of Prophets' Superior Intelligence

It is a well-known fact that the intelligence of prophets surpasses all others. Therefore, I (Ibn Jawzi) did not want my book to be devoid of this.

Isma'il (peace be upon him)

Said b. Jubayr and Ibn Abbas (Allah be pleased with him) narrate: Isma'il (peace be upon him) married a woman from the Jurhum tribe. One day, his father Ibrahim (peace be upon him) visited him but did not find him at home. His wife said, "He went out to provide for us." When Ibrahim (peace be upon him) asked about their livelihood, she told him they were in poverty and distress. Upon leaving, Ibrahim (peace be upon him) advised her, "When your husband returns, convey my greetings to him and have him change the threshold of his house." When Isma'il (peace be upon him) returned and learned of this, he said to his wife, "The visitor was my father, and he wants me to divorce you. Get up, return to your family!" This incident demonstrates how intelligent Isma'il (peace be upon him) was.

Sulayman (peace be upon him)

- Abu Hurairah (Allah be pleased with him) narrates from the Prophet (peace and blessings of Allah be upon him): "Two women set out on a journey with their two children. Along the way, a wolf attacked and killed one of the children. The women disputed over who should claim the surviving child. They brought their case to Prophet Dawud (peace be upon him), who decided to give the child to the elder woman. However, they later went to Sulayman (peace be upon him) and explained the situation. Sulayman (peace be upon him) ordered, 'Bring me a knife; I will divide the child into two and give each of you half.' Upon hearing this, the younger woman said, 'Will you divide him into two? Then I withdraw my claim; let the child be with her.' Thus, Sulayman (peace be upon him) said, 'He belongs to you,' and gave the child to the younger woman.

- Abdullah b. Ubayd b. Umeyr narrates: Sulayman (peace be upon him) sent his army to fetch a rebellious jinn. When the jinn arrived at the palace, he picked up a stick from the ground, measured the distance, and threw it towards the room where Sulayman (peace be upon him) was. When asked about this, Sulayman's officials reported the incident. Sulayman (peace be upon him) explained, "Do you know what this means? It means 'Do as you wish! Eventually, you will end up under so much ground.'"

- Muhammad b. Ka'b al-Qurani narrates: A man came to Sulayman (peace be upon him) claiming that his neighbor had stolen his geese. Sulayman (peace be upon him) gathered the people in the mosque, ascended the pulpit, and declared, "Among you is one who not only steals his neighbor's geese but also comes to the mosque with their feathers on his head!" Hearing this, a man in the congregation nervously scratched his head. Sulayman (peace be upon him) declared, "Seize him! This is the thief."

Isa (peace be upon him) and Satan

One day, Satan approached Isa (peace be upon him) and said, "You claim that nothing can happen to you except what Allah has decreed. So, climb up that mountain and throw yourself down! If it is decreed for you to be saved, you will survive." Isa (peace be upon him) responded, "O accursed one! Allah can test His servants, but the servants have no right to test Allah the Exalted."

Narratives from Previous Generations

L ukman (peace be upon him)

Makhool narrates: "Lukman (peace be upon him) was a dark-skinned man to whom Allah had granted wisdom. He was a slave purchased by an Israelite for 120 grams of gold. His master was an habitual gambler and had a river flowing in front of his house. One day, he played a game of backgammon with another man under the condition that the loser must either drink all the river's water or pay a heavy penalty. His master lost. The winner demanded, 'Either drink the water or pay the price!' His master replied, 'I can't drink the water; let me pay the price. What do you want?' The man responded, 'Either I gouge out your eyes or you give me all your wealth and property. One of these two choices.' His master asked for 24 hours to fulfill the demand and went home distressed.

In the evening, Lukman (peace be upon him) came back carrying a bundle of firewood on his back and greeted his master. After setting down the wood, Lukman's master, who often mocked him but always received wise and kind responses, saw Lukman and sat down next to him. Lukman noticed his master was troubled and said, 'You look upset.' His master turned away without responding. Lukman repeated his concern three times, each time receiving the same dismissive response. Finally, Lukman said, 'If you tell me what happened, maybe I can help you find a solution.' His master then explained the situation.

Lukman (peace be upon him) reassured him, 'Do not worry! There is a solution.' When his master asked what it was, Lukman explained: 'When the man comes tomorrow, tell him, "I want to drink the river's water, but should I drink what flows between the banks or the entire flow?" He will tell you to drink what is between the banks. Then you say, "Stop the flow so I can drink it." Since he can't stop the river from flowing, you will have fulfilled your obligation.'

His master found the advice sensible and was relieved. The next morning, when the man came to claim his due, the master asked, 'Shall I drink the flowing water or what is between the banks?' The man responded, 'Drink what is between the banks.' The master then said, 'Stop the flow so I can drink it,' effectively nullifying the demand since the man couldn't stop the river. Following this, the master was so impressed by Lukman's wisdom that he freed him."

These stories highlight the profound wisdom and intelligence bestowed upon the prophets and wise men, demonstrating their extraordinary ability to solve complex problems and face challenges with clarity and insight.

Lukman's Advice to His Son

According to the narration of Muhammad b. Ishaq, Lukman (peace be upon him) advised his son, "O my son! When you wish to make someone your friend, first anger them. If, in their anger, they still act fairly towards you, then make them your friend; if not, be wary of them."

Abdullah b. Amir al-Azdi and the People of Saba'

The Gardens of Saba' and Their Downfall

Dahhaak narrated from Ibn Abbas (Allah be pleased with him): "The people of Saba' in Yemen had gardens so lush that they resembled paradise in both summer and winter. Despite these blessings, they fell into disbelief. Consequently, Allah sent rats with iron teeth and claws to gnaw at the dam they had built. The first to notice this was Abdullah b. Amir al-Azdi. One day, he saw these rats gnawing at the dam with their iron claws and teeth. He returned home and informed his family. He then sent his children to confirm what he had seen, asking them, 'Did you see what I saw?' They replied, 'Yes, we saw it too.' Abdullah said, 'There is nothing we can do. This is Allah's will.'

He even brought a cat to the site, but the rats were unfazed, and the cat fled in fear. Realizing a disaster was imminent, Abdullah decided he could no longer live among such a people and devised a plan to leave.

Abdullah's Plan to Leave

Abdullah instructed his children, 'Tomorrow, when we are in the assembly - where my words are respected - I will give the youngest of you a task. Delay in carrying out the task until I become angry, and then slap me. You, the elder siblings, will remain silent. The people in the assembly will also be hesitant to intervene. I will then stand up and say, "If my youngest child can slap me, and none of you react, I cannot live among you any longer!"'

The following day, they executed the plan. The youngest child slapped Abdullah when he became angry. His siblings stayed silent, and the assembly members did not intervene. Abdullah then stood up and swore, 'If my youngest child can slap me, and you don't even flinch, I cannot live here!' The assembly members apologized, saying, 'We did not intervene because we assumed your children would handle it.' Abdullah replied, 'It's too late now; I cannot stay here another moment. I have no choice but to leave.' He then sold all his possessions. The people competed to buy his belongings. After selling everything, Abdullah left with his family.

Shortly thereafter, the rats completely destroyed the dam. One night, while everyone was asleep, the waters broke through, sweeping away their wealth, livestock, and homes..."

Narratives Indicating the Wisdom and Intelligence of Our Prophet (Peace and blessings of Allah be upon him)

Clever Strategies and Responses

Harise b. Muzrib's narrative of the Battle of Badr

Harise b. Muzrib narrates from Ali (Allah be pleased with him): "When we arrived at Badr, we found two men. One was a Qurayshite, and the other was Ukba b. Abi Muayt's freed slave. The Qurayshite fled, and we captured Ukba's freed slave. We asked him, 'How many are the enemy?' He kept saying, 'By Allah, they are many and strong!' When he repeated this, the Muslims beat him. Eventually, we brought him to the Prophet (peace and blessings of Allah be upon him). The Prophet asked, 'How many are they?' He replied again, 'By Allah, they are many and strong!' He would not give a specific number no matter how much he was pressed. Then, the Prophet (peace and blessings of Allah be upon him) tried another approach and asked him how many camels they slaughtered daily. The man said, 'They slaughter ten camels every day.' The Prophet then concluded, 'They are about a thousand men, since one camel serves one hundred people.'"

Ka'b b. Malik on the Prophet's Military Tactics

Ka'b b. Malik narrated that whenever the Prophet (peace and blessings of Allah be upon him) planned to go to war, he would give the impression of heading to a different destination.

Practical Wisdom and Dealing with Adversity

Abu Sa'id al-Khudri on the Prohibition of Alcohol

Abu Sa'id al-Khudri (Allah be pleased with him) narrated: "When the first verses about alcohol were revealed, the Prophet (peace and blessings of Allah be upon him) said, 'Allah condemns alcohol; a decree concerning it will soon come. Whoever has any alcohol should sell it or benefit from it in some way.' Shortly afterward, a brief verse came saying, 'Allah has forbidden alcohol. Anyone who possesses it should neither drink it nor sell it!' Consequently, people poured out all their alcohol into the streets of Medina."

On Handling Interruptions During Prayer

Aisha (Allah be pleased with him), the beloved wife of the Prophet (peace and blessings of Allah be upon him), reported that the Prophet (peace and blessings of Allah be upon him) said, 'If someone's ablution is broken during prayer, let them hold their nose and exit.'

On Handling Difficult Neighbors

Abu Huraira (Allah be pleased with him) recounted: "A man complained to the Prophet (peace and blessings of Allah be upon him) about his troublesome neighbor. The Prophet (peace and blessings of Allah be upon him) advised, 'Go and place all your belongings in the street.' The man did so. People asked him, 'What is going on?' He replied, 'My neighbor has been causing me trouble. I informed the Messenger of Allah (peace and blessings of Allah be upon him), and he advised me to take my belongings outside.' Hearing this, people began to curse the troublesome neighbor, saying, 'O Allah, disgrace him!' The neighbor, overwhelmed by the public reaction, came to the man and promised, 'Return to your home. I swear by Allah, I will never trouble you again.'"

Reflections on the Prophet's Companions

Zayd b. Aslam on the Companions' Admiration

Zayd b. Aslam narrated: "A man said to Huzayfa, 'O Huzayfa! We envy your companionship with the Prophet (peace and blessings of Allah be upon him). You were fortunate to be with him, but we never got the chance to see him.' Huzayfa (Allah be pleased with him) replied, 'We envy your faith without seeing him. My dear brother, how would you have been if you had seen the Prophet (peace and blessings of Allah be upon him)?' He then recounted: 'During the Battle of the Trench, we were with the Prophet (peace and blessings of Allah be upon him) on a dark, cold, and rainy night. Abu Sufyan and his army had camped outside Madinah. The Prophet (peace and blessings of Allah be upon him) declared, "Whoever brings information about them, Allah will grant him a place in Paradise on the Day of Judgment!" None of us moved. He repeated, "Whoever brings information about them, may Allah make him my companion on the Day of Judgment!" Again, no one moved. The third time, he said, "Whoever brings information about them, Allah will place him alongside me on the Day of Judgment!" Still, no one moved. Finally, Abu Bakr (Allah be pleased with him) suggested, "O Messenger of Allah, let Huzayfa go!" The Prophet (peace and blessings of Allah be upon him) called me. I responded, "May my parents be sacrificed for you! What is your command?" He asked, "Will you go?" I replied, "I am not afraid of death but fear being captured." The Prophet (peace and blessings of Allah be upon him) assured me, "You will not be captured." I then said, "Command me, and I will go!" He instructed, "Go and infiltrate their ranks. First, go to the Quraysh and say, 'O Quraysh, indeed the people are planning to say tomorrow, where is Quraysh? Where are the leaders of the people? Where are the heads of the people? They want to put you in the forefront so you will engage in the fighting first.' Then, go to the Qays and tell them, 'O Qais, tomorrow people will ask, "Where are the cavalry? Where are the horsemen?" They will put you in the forefront so you will bear the brunt of the fighting!'"

Blending in with the Enemy

"I went and mingled among them. Sitting by the fire with them, I began spreading these words."

Abu Sufyan's Caution

As the night progressed, Abu Sufyan stood up and prayed to Lat and Uzza. Then he said, "Everyone, check who is sitting next to you!" Someone was sitting next to me. Without giving him a chance to recognize me, I grabbed him and asked, 'Who are you?' He replied, 'I am so-and-so, son of so-and-so.' I said, 'Very well.'"

Panic Among the Enemy

As dawn approached, people started shouting, 'Where is Quraysh? Where is the leader of the people, Quraysh? Fulfill the commitments you made yesterday!' 'Where is Bani Kinana? Are the archers ready? Come on, fulfill your responsibilities!' And so, they began to argue amongst themselves."

Divine Intervention

"Allah Almighty sent a fierce wind that night. It left no tent standing, nor any pots and pans in place. I saw Abu Sufyan thrown on his tethered camel, unable to pull it up because he could not stand."

Reporting Back to the Prophet

"I returned to the Prophet (peace and blessings of Allah be upon him) and narrated what had happened and described the state of Abu Sufyan. The Prophet (peace and blessings of Allah be upon him) laughed until his molar teeth were visible."

The Prophet's (peace and blessings of Allah be upon him) Justice and Mercy

A Man Brings His Friend's Killer to the Prophet

Asim al-Ahwal narrated from Hasan al-Basri: "A man brought the killer of his friend to the Prophet (peace and blessings of Allah be upon him). The Messenger of Allah (peace and blessings of Allah be upon him) asked him, 'Do you want to accept blood money?' The man replied, 'No, I do not.'"

Considering Forgiveness

"The Prophet (peace and blessings of Allah be upon him) then asked, 'Can you forgive him?' The man replied, 'No, I cannot forgive him.' The Prophet (peace and blessings of Allah be upon him) then said, 'In that case, take him away and kill him.'"

A Call for Mercy

"After the man left, the Prophet (peace and blessings of Allah be upon him) said, 'If he kills him, then he is like him.' Hearing this, one of the companions ran after them and said, 'The Messenger of Allah (peace and blessings of Allah be upon him) says this and that.' On hearing this, the man released the killer whom he was dragging by his collar."

Ibn Qutayba's Explanation

Ibn Qutayba explains: "The Prophet (peace and blessings of Allah be upon him) did not mean that the man would commit the same sin and end up in Hell if he executed the killer. Since Allah has permitted retribution, this could not be the meaning. Instead, the Prophet (peace and blessings of Allah be upon him) was emphasizing his desire for the man to forgive the killer. By saying, 'If he kills him, then he is like him,' he implied that the act of killing remains an act of killing. Both are killers, but the first is a wrongdoer, and the second is executing justice. The Prophet's intention was to encourage forgiveness."

Numerous Teachings on Justice and Mercy

The Prophet (peace and blessings of Allah be upon him) had many sayings of this kind. We suffice with narrating just this one here.

Narratives from the Companions of the Prophet (peace and blessings of Allah be upon him)

———

Abu Bakr's (RA) Role during the Hijrah

Anas (RA) narrated: "During the Hijrah, the Prophet (peace and blessings of Allah be upon him) was riding his mount, and Abu Bakr was following behind him. Despite knowing the route very well due to his frequent travels to Sham, Abu Bakr (Allah be pleased with him), when recognized by the people of the villages they passed, and asked, 'O Abu Bakr! Who is this man with you?' He would reply, 'He is my guide showing me the way.'"

The Story of Abu Bakr's Understanding

The Prophet's Last Public Speech

Hasan al-Basri narrated: "The Prophet Muhammad (peace and blessings of Allah be upon him) went out with Abu Bakr to address the people shortly before his passing. He said, 'Allah has given a servant the choice between this world and the Hereafter, and the servant has chosen the Hereafter.' Upon hearing this, Abu Bakr began to weep. We were surprised by his tears, but Abu Bakr was the only one among us who understood that the servant referred to was the Prophet Muhammad himself."

Umar's Acts of Leadership

Umar's Response to the War Incentive

Offering Incentives for Battle

Buraid's father, Jarir, recounts: "When people were stirred up to fight against the Persians in Iraq, Umar called me and said, 'If you go with your people and achieve victory, a quarter of the spoils will be yours!' After the battle, I reminded Sa'd of Umar's promise. Sa'd wrote to Umar about it, and Umar replied, 'Jarir is right; I made this offer to him. If he and his people fought for what was promised, give it to them. But if they fought for Allah, His religion, and His Prophet, then they should receive the same as the rest of the Muslims.'"

Jarir's Noble Decision

"After reading Umar's letter, Jarir said, 'I don't need the quarter. I am just one of the Muslims,' and he relinquished his claim to the additional share of the spoils."

Umar's Keen Insight

Identifying a Soothsayer

Nafi' narrated from Ibn Umar: "One day, Umar was sitting when he saw a man. Umar remarked, 'If that man is not a soothsayer, then I lack discernment.' They called the man over, and Umar asked him, 'Are you a soothsayer?' The man replied, 'Yes.'"

Choosing Kind Words

Umar was walking through the city one night and saw a fire burning in a hollow place. He felt it inappropriate to address the people as 'O people of the fire!' So instead, he called out, 'O people of the light!' This choice of words demonstrated Umar's thoughtful and considerate nature.

Umar's Advice on Giving Blessings

"It is also narrated that Umar once asked a man who had just gotten married, 'Did anyone wish you well?' The man replied, 'No, and may Allah not prolong your life.' Umar responded, 'You should have said,

'No, may Allah prolong your life.' From this, we learn the importance of speaking with kindness and blessings.'"

Stories about Ali ibn Abi Talib (Allah be pleased with him)

Ali's Humble Response to Praise

"Abu al-Bakhtari narrated: 'A man came to Ali ibn Abi Talib and praised him excessively while harboring enmity in his heart. Ali responded, 'I am not as you say, but I am better than what is in your heart.'"

Ali's Wisdom in Judgment

The Case of the Lost Deposit

Hanbash ibn Mu'tamir narrates: "Two men entrusted a woman from Quraysh with 100 dinars, instructing her, 'Do not give this money to either of us unless we both come together.' After a year, one of the men came to the woman and said, 'My friend has died, so give me the money.' She refused, saying, 'You both told me not to give it unless you were together.'"

The Woman Under Pressure

"The man, using his family and neighbors, pressured the woman until she reluctantly handed over the money. A year later, the other man returned and asked for the money. The woman explained what had happened. The man took her to Umar to complain. Sensing the woman was trapped, she pleaded, 'For Allah's sake, O Umar, send us to Ali!'"

Ali's Wise Ruling

"Umar then referred the case to Ali, who realized they had deceived her. After hearing the case, Ali asked the man, 'Didn't you both say, "Do not give the money to either of us unless we both come together?"' When he confirmed, Ali said, 'Then your money is with us. Bring your companion, and we will give it to you both.'"

Wise Judgments of Ali ibn Abi Talib (RA)

A Solution for an Oath During Ramadan

"Muhammad narrates from his father: A man came to Ali and said, 'I have sworn that if I do not engage in intercourse with my wife during the day in Ramadan, she will be divorced from me with three divorces.' Ali replied, 'Travel with her so that you are not obliged to fast during the day while on a journey. Thus, you may engage in intercourse during the day in Ramadan.'"

The Wisdom and Insight of Hasan ibn Ali (Allah be pleased with him)

Ibn Muljam's Attempt to Deceive Hasan

"Abu al-Wafa ibn Aqil writes: When the killer of Ali, Ibn Muljam, was brought before Hasan, he said, 'I wish to whisper something into your ear.' Hasan replied, 'He wants to bite my ear,' and refused to let him come close. Ibn Muljam then confessed, 'Indeed, if he had let me, I would have bitten off his earlobe.' Ibn Aqil continues, 'Observe the wisdom of Hasan; even amidst a calamity that would overwhelm anyone, he remained vigilant. And look at the cursed Ibn Muljam; despite his dire situation, he still sought to deceive.'"

The Integrity and Fairness of Husayn ibn Ali (Allah be pleased with him)

Husayn and the False Claim

"Ibrahim ibn Riyah al-Mawsili recounts: A man falsely claimed that Husayn owed him money and took him to the judge. Husayn said, 'Let him swear by Allah and take what he claims.' The man began his oath with, 'By Allah, besides whom there is no deity...' Husayn interrupted and said, 'Just say, "By Allah, by Allah, by Allah, this claim is rightfully mine.'" The man complied, and as he was leaving, his legs faltered, and he fell dead. When asked why he insisted on that specific wording, Husayn replied, 'I wanted to elevate the name of Allah such that He would not be lenient towards someone who swears falsely.'"

The Humility and Insight of Abbas ibn Abdul-Muttalib (Allah be pleased with him)

"Abu Razin narrates: Abbas was asked, 'Are you older, or is the Prophet (peace and blessings of Allah be upon him) older?' Abbas replied, 'He is greater than me, but I was born before him.'"

Advice to the Prophet After the Battle of Badr

"Ikrima reports from Ibn Abbas: When the battle of Badr was won, it was suggested to the Prophet, 'You should seize the Quraysh caravan from Syria; there is nothing left to prevent you.' Abbas ibn Abdul Muttalib, who was then a prisoner in chains, called out, 'It is not suitable for you to do so.' The Prophet asked, 'Why not?' Abbas replied, 'Because Allah, the Exalted, has promised you one of the two groups (either the caravan or the army), and He has already fulfilled His promise with the victory at Badr.'"

Acts of Compassion and Respect

Handling Embarrassment with Wisdom

The Prophet's Approach to Cleanliness

"Mujahid narrates: The Prophet (peace and blessings of Allah be upon him) was with his companions when he sensed an unpleasant odor. He said, 'Whoever is responsible for this odor should get up and perform ablution.' The person was too embarrassed to move. The Prophet repeated, 'Whoever is responsible should perform ablution; Allah does not shy away from the truth.' Abbas then suggested, 'Let us all perform ablution together so that the person can perform ablution without feeling embarrassed.' The Prophet agreed, saying, 'Indeed, Allah does not shy away from the truth.'"

Umar ibn al-Khattab's Similar Act of Kindness

"A similar incident occurred with Umar ibn al-Khattab (Allah be pleased with him). During a gathering that included Jarir ibn Abdullah, a foul odor was noticed. Umar said, 'Whoever is responsible should perform ablution.' Jarir ibn Abdullah suggested, 'O Commander of the Faithful, let us all perform ablution together to spare the individual from embarrassment.' Umar replied, 'May Allah have mercy on you, Jarir! You are as noble in Islam as you were during the days of ignorance (pre-Islamic period).'"

The Steadfastness of the Companions

Seeking Volunteers to Confront an Enemy of Islam

"Jabir (RA) narrates: One day, the Prophet (peace and blessings of Allah be upon him) asked, 'Who will deal with Ka'b ibn al-Ashraf? He has caused harm to Allah and His Messenger.' Muhammad ibn Maslama volunteered.

Muhammad ibn Maslama and the Assassination of Ka'b ibn al-Ashraf

A Bold Proposal

Muhammad ibn Maslama approached the Prophet (peace and blessings of Allah be upon him) and said, 'O Messenger of Allah, do you want me to deal with Ka'b ibn al-Ashraf?' The Prophet replied, 'Yes, I do.' Muhammad ibn Maslama then said, 'Allow me to speak ill of you to deceive him.' The Prophet (peace and blessings of Allah be upon him) permitted him to do so."

Deceiving the Enemy

"Muhammad ibn Maslama went to Ka'b ibn al-Ashraf and said, 'This man (referring to the Prophet) has taken all our wealth as charity and has caused us great hardship. We are fed up with him.' Ka'b responded, 'I suspected this would happen.' They continued their conversation:

- 'Indeed, but we need to understand his plans and see the outcome before we hand him over to you. After all, we followed him for a reason. Now, we need some dates on credit from you.'

- 'I can give you the dates, but you must provide collateral. Perhaps your women as security?'

- 'How can we mortgage our women while you are the most handsome of the Arabs?'

- 'Then your children as security.'

- 'No, since people will scorn us for that. Our children will curse us if we offer them as security for a few measures of dates.'

Ka'b then asked, 'So what will you offer as security?'

- 'We will give our weapons as security.'

Muhammad ibn Maslama agreed to bring the weapons and left."

Executing the Plan

"Muhammad ibn Maslama returned with Ka'b's foster brother, Abu Na'ila, and two other men. He hid them among the date palms and instructed them, 'When I grab Ka'b and seize his head, you attack and kill him.' He then called out to Ka'b, who prepared to leave his house. Ka'b's wife asked, 'Where are you going at this hour?' Ka'b replied, 'It's Muhammad ibn Maslama and my brother, Abu Na'ila!'

Ka'b wore a single garment and was perfumed."

Luring Ka'b to His Fate

"Muhammad ibn Maslama praised his scent, to which Ka'b boasted, 'Of course, I smell good. I have the best perfume, and beside me is the daughter of so-and-so, the most fragrant woman among the Arabs.' Muhammad ibn Maslama asked to smell the fragrance more closely, and when Ka'b consented, he grabbed his head with both hands and signaled, 'Attack the enemy of Allah!' The men then leaped upon Ka'b and killed him. They returned to inform the Prophet (peace and blessings of Allah be upon him) of their success."

The Wisdom of Muawiya ibn Abi Sufyan

Muawiya's Philosophy on Trust

"Rabia ibn Najid narrates: When asked, 'What is the pinnacle of your wisdom?' Muawiya ibn Abi Sufyan replied, 'To trust no one completely.'"

A Claim of Brotherhood with Muawiyah

A Man Approaches Muawiyah's Gatekeeper

An Arab man came to the gatekeeper of Muawiyah and instructed him to say to Muawiyah: "Your brother from the same mother and father has come."

Muawiyah responded: "I do not know him; let him in."

When the man entered, the following conversation took place:

The Question of Kinship

Muawiyah asked: "How are you my brother?"

The man replied: "From Adam and Eve."

Muawiyah said: "Give him a dirham!"

The man protested: "Are you giving only one dirham to your brother from the same mother and father?"

The Reply on Brotherhood

Muawiyah answered: "If I were to give one dirham to every brother I have from Adam and Eve, you wouldn't even get this much!"

Mughirah ibn Shu'bah and the Young Suitor

A Competition for a Woman's Hand

Sabih al-Kufi narrated: "Mughirah ibn Shu'bah and a young man both sought to marry a woman."

The young man was also handsome. The woman wrote a letter saying: "Both of you desire me, but I cannot give an answer until I see and talk to you. Come to me if you wish!"

They went to her. The woman seated them before her. Mughirah noticed the young man's good looks and eloquence, fearing that the woman would prefer him.

The Woman's Question and the Young Man's Response

The woman asked the young man: "You have beauty, handsomeness, and eloquence. Do you have any other qualities?"

The young man listed many of his virtues and then fell silent.

The woman then asked: "How are you with accounting?"

The young man replied: "Nothing escapes my account. I even account for a small mustard seed."

Mughirah's Clever Intervention

Taking advantage of this, Mughirah interjected: "As for me, I place the moneybag in a corner of the house. My family spends as they wish. I do not check whether it is empty or not. When it runs out, I fill it without any account."

The Woman's Decision

The woman concluded: "This elder who does not keep an account of the spending is better than the handsome young man who accounts for even a mustard seed."

She then married Mughirah.

The Wisdom of Amr ibn al-As

The Conquest of Caesarea and the Governor's Request

Ibn al-Kalbi narrated: "When Amr ibn al-As conquered Caesarea and reached Gaza, the governor sent a letter saying: 'Send me a man from among your companions so that I can speak to him.'"

Amr thought and said: "No one should go but me."

Amr's Interaction with the Governor

Amr went and spoke with the governor. The governor was greatly impressed by his eloquence and asked: "Are there others like you among your companions?"

Amr's Humble Response

Amr replied: "You can judge my lack of worth among them by the fact that they sent me to you and exposed me to what you might do, not knowing what you would decide."

The governor instructed that gifts and money be given to him. He ordered the gatekeeper to strike his neck and take back what had been given when Amr left the gate.

Amr had not yet reached the gate when he encountered a Christian from the Gassan tribe. The man warned him, "Make sure to leave as securely as you entered!"

Upon hearing this, Amr turned back and went before the governor again. When the governor asked, "Why did you return?" he replied, "I thought to bring more gifts to you and want your permission to go and come back to you with lots of gifts."

The governor became happy, "You speak the truth. Go and bring them quickly!" He instructed the gatekeeper to open the gate and not to follow the previous command.

Amr left, keeping watch around him. When he was far from the place of danger, he vowed to himself never to do such a thing again.

Later, when they met face to face to make peace, the governor said, "Is that you?" Amr (may Allah be pleased with him) responded, "Despite your treachery, it is me."

Huzaym b. Sabit (may Allah be pleased with him)

Huzeyme al-Ansari narrated from his uncle: "The Prophet (peace be upon him) purchased a horse from a Bedouin. Since the Bedouin had no money with him, the Prophet asked him to accompany him home. They set out, with the Prophet walking briskly and the Bedouin trailing behind. Along the way, some people unaware that the horse was already sold approached the Bedouin and bargained, offering more than what the Prophet had given. Upon this, the Bedouin called out from behind, 'Either buy it or I will sell it!' The Prophet asked, 'Did I not buy it?' The Bedouin replied, 'No, you did not!' As they were talking, people gathered around. The Bedouin insisted, 'Bring a witness that I sold it to you!' The Muslims present said, 'Shame on you! The Messenger of Allah does not lie.' But the Bedouin persisted. Then Huzeyme arrived, heard the defense of the Prophet and the Bedouin, and without hesitation said, 'I bear witness.' The Prophet (peace be upon him) asked him, 'What are you testifying to, O Huzeyme?' He replied, 'I testify to your truthfulness, O Messenger of Allah!'"

In another narration, when the Prophet asked, 'Were you with us?' Huzeyme replied, 'We believe in what you brought from Allah (from the heavens). Shouldn't we believe in what you say here?'

Other accounts of Intelligence

Hisham ibn Abd al-Malik

Hisham said to his son's tutor: "If my son were to do something wrong or say something inappropriate among the believers, do not rebuke him in front of people lest he becomes embarrassed. Correcting his mistake publicly might lead to his persistence in error. Cover his fault at that moment and only reprimand him when you are alone."

Caliph al-Saffah

Sa'id al-Bahili's father narrated: "Al-Saffah of the Banu Hashim was jealous of the Shi'ites and the prominent people. One day, Abdullah ibn Hussein ibn Hasan came to him with a Qur'an in his hand and said, 'O Commander of the Believers, give us our right as decreed by Allah in this Qur'an!' Those present wondered whether al-Saffah would do something to this elderly man or give him a disdainful answer. However, al-Saffah calmly turned to him and said, 'Your grandfather Ali (may Allah be pleased with him) was more righteous and just than me, and he was appointed to lead in this matter. This right was given to your forefathers Hasan and Hussein, who were better than you. Therefore, today I must give you the same right. If I were to give more, it would not be justice but excess.' Abdullah left without saying a word, and people admired al-Saffah's response."

Caliph al-Mansur

Ismail ibn Muhammad relates: "Caliph Mansur asked Ibn Herime who had come to him, 'What is your request?' Ibn Herime replied, 'Write to the governor of Madinah not to punish me if he sees me drunk!' When Mansur said it was impossible to cancel this punishment, Ibn

Herime insisted, 'I have no other request; this is all I want.' Thereupon, the Caliph ordered, 'Write to the governor of Madinah: if Ibn Herime is found drunk, he should receive eighty lashes, and the one who brings him should receive a hundred lashes.' After this, the police would release Ibn Herime asking, 'Who will exchange eighty for a hundred?'

One day, Caliph Mansur was sitting in a high place in the city when he saw a man rushing anxiously through the streets. He sent someone to bring him to his presence and asked about his situation. The man explained that he had given the money earned from trading to his wife, and even though there were no signs of theft at home, his wife claimed the money was stolen. Their conversation continued:

- How long have you been married?

- A year.

- Was she a virgin?

- No.

- Does she have children from someone else?

- No.

- Is she young or old?

- Young.

Upon this, the Caliph gave the man a bottle containing a pleasant and strong fragrance and said, "Apply this; your distress will pass." Then he sent four of his men to the four gates of the city with instructions, "If anyone smells this fragrance on someone, seize him and bring him to me!" Meanwhile, the man returned home and gave the bottle to his wife, saying, "The caliph gave this to me as a gift." His wife admired the scent greatly and sent it to the man she loved and to whom she previously gave her husband's money, saying, "The caliph gave this to my husband; use it." The man applied the fragrance. Later, as he was leaving the city gate, the guards caught him and brought him to Caliph Mansur. Mansur asked where he got the fragrance. The man said he bought it. When Mansur asked whom he bought it from, the man became flustered and confused. Thereupon, the caliph called the guard and ordered, "Take this man; if he brings the full amount of dinars, let him go; if not, give him a thousand lashes without hesitation." Faced with the difficulty, the man agreed to bring the dinars. When the situation was reported to him, Mansur summoned the owner of the dinars and said, "If I return your money exactly as it is, will you accept my ruling regarding your wife?" The man agreed, "Yes, I will." Mansur then said, "In that case, your wife is divorced!" and explained what had happened.

The Fake Sandal of the Prophet

The Gift of the Sandal:

Muhammad bin Al-Fadl reported from a literate person about Hasan al-Waseef: "Al-Mahdi sat in public for the people, and a man entered with a sandal wrapped in a cloth."

The man said: "O Commander of the Faithful, this is the sandal of the Prophet (peace be upon him), which I am presenting to you as a gift."

Al-Mahdi said: "Let me see it." He took the sandal, kissed its sole, and placed it on his eyes. He then ordered the man to be given ten thousand dirhams.

After the man received the money and left, Al-Mahdi turned to his companions and said: "Do you think I didn't know that the Prophet (peace be upon him) never saw this sandal, let alone wore it? But if we had called him a liar, he would have told the people that he brought the sandal of the Prophet to the Commander of the Faithful, and he rejected it. More people would have believed him than denied his story."

Strategic Wisdom:

Al-Mahdi explained: "Given that the general public tends to support the weaker party against the stronger, even if the weaker is in the wrong, we chose to buy his silence, accept his gift, and affirm his story. We believed that this action was the most successful and beneficial course."

Caliph Mu'tadid's Nighttime Encounter

A Grim Discovery:

Al-Muhsin narrates: "One night, Caliph Mu'tadid went out for some personal reason. He saw a few youths standing over the body of a freshly murdered child. At that moment, the killer was from among them."

Caliph's Investigation:

"Mu'tadid approached them and checked each of their hearts one by one. He noticed that one of their hearts was beating very rapidly. He pushed him with his foot, and with a little pressure, the youth confessed to the crime."

A Gruesome Find at the Tigris

The Fisherman's Find:

Again, Al-Muhsin recounts: "One day, one of Mu'tadid's servants came to him and said, 'While sitting by the Tigris today, I saw a fisherman. At one point, he struggled with something heavy, and a large bag emerged from his net. The man thought it was filled with gold, but it contained a severed hand.' The servant showed the severed hand to the Caliph."

Further Investigation:

The Caliph ordered that nets be cast around the area where the hand was found. This time, a bag with a severed foot was retrieved. Although they continued to search, nothing else was found.

Disturbed, the Caliph said, "Someone is killing people, dismembering them in my city, and I am unaware of it." That day, he neither ate nor drank anything.

Tracing the Bag's Origin:

The next day, he called a trusted person, handed him the bag, and instructed: "Find out who in Baghdad makes these bags. When you find the weaver, ask who bought them. Do not inform anyone and come directly to me!"

Bag Maker in Baghdad

Three days later, the man came back. He said he had visited all the weavers and finally found the one who made the bags. He explained:

The Weaver's Revelation

"The weaver said he sold these bags to a perfumer in Yahya Bazaar. When the perfumer saw the bag, he exclaimed, 'Oh no! Where did you get this?' I asked if he recognized the bag. 'Yes, a Hashimi bought about ten bags three days ago. I don't know why he bought them, but this is one of them!' he said.

Identifying the Hashimi

When I asked, 'Who is this Hashimi?' he replied, 'He is one of the Ali b. Reyta's descendants. His name is so-and-so. He is the most oppressive and wicked among people. He violates the sanctity of Muslim households and loves to set traps for them. Everyone knows him, but no one dares to inform Caliph Mu'tazid because they fear his malice. Let me tell you his story:

The Tale of the Captive Singer

For several years, this man loved a singer who was as beautiful as a moonbeam and as finely crafted as a coin. He wanted to buy her from her master, but the master wouldn't even let him come close. A few days ago, he heard that the master put the singer up for sale and someone had offered thousands of dinars for her. He sent a message requesting to bid her farewell before she was sold. The master sent her over since he was threatened by him. He kept her in his house for three days and then seized her. Since then, no news has been heard. Some say the singer escaped, some say he is holding her in his house, and others claim he killed her. The mourning master went to his door several times but got nothing.'

Caliph Mu'tazid's Justice

When Caliph Mu'tazid heard these things, he prostrated in thanks because the criminal was exposed. He immediately had the Hashimi captured and rescued the singer. The severed hand and foot were shown. Upon seeing them, the Hashimi turned pale and, realizing his end was near, confessed his crime. The Caliph ordered that the singer's value be paid to her master from the state treasury and imprisoned the Hashimi. It's said he was either executed or kept in prison until he died.

Yahya's Advice to His Son:

"Yahya advised his son, 'My son! Try to learn a little of every knowledge. A person tends to be hostile towards things they do not know. I do not want you to be hostile towards any knowledge. Whoever attains a position and loses themselves there does not belong there; they belong to a lower place.'"

Avoiding Arrogance:

"When someone told him, 'You are wiser than Ahmed,' Yahya replied, 'I do not associate with those who overestimate my worth.'"

Words of Caution by Fazl ibn Rabi:

"Fazl ibn Rabi advised, 'Avoid saying things to kings that would require them to respond; if they respond, it will be harsh on them, and if they do not, it will be heavy on you.'"

Generosity Redefined:

"Salab reported, 'When I told Hasan ibn Sahl that there is no good in extravagance due to his frequent generosity, he replied, 'On the contrary, there is no extravagance in doing good.'"

A Diplomatic Solution:

"When Fath ibn Hakan saw something in Khalif Al-Mutawakkil's beard, he neither removed it nor warned him. Instead, he said to the servant, 'Bring the mirror for the Commander of the Faithful!'"

Serving with Loyalty

Service to Hasan ibn Furat:

"Abu Ali ibn Makula narrates, 'I was a scribe in the service of Hasan ibn Furat, earning ten dinars a month. He was overseeing his brother's duties and, when his situation improved, he raised my salary to thirty dinars.'"

"'I stayed with him until he became the first minister. When he became the minister, he increased my salary to five hundred dinars.'"

Integrity in Difficult Times

Handling Confiscated Goods:

"Once, Hasan ibn Furat ordered the confiscation of the properties of the rebels allied with Ibn al-Mu'tazz. After inspecting the confiscated items, he would send them to the treasury of Al-Muqtadir."

"One day, two chests were brought, claiming they were found in the house of Ibn al-Mu'tazz. When he asked what was inside, they said it contained the names of his supporters."

"Hasan ordered, 'Do not open them!' and instructed the servants to burn the chests. This decision was bold and definitive, demonstrating his commitment to the state's integrity."

Turning to those present in the assembly, he said, 'If I had even glanced at those lists, everyone whose name was on them would think I had learned of their intentions against me and the caliph. This would not be appropriate behavior.'" "After the chests had completely burned, he turned to me and said, 'O Abu Ali! I have issued a pardon for everyone associated with Ibn al-Mu'tazz. Write a general amnesty decree covering all the opponents. I appoint you to handle this task.'" "He further instructed, 'Spread the word among the people what I have told you, so that those in hiding can come forward and be included in the amnesty!' We thanked him, and the news spread, leading to a general amnesty."

Tale of Intrigue and Loyalty

Exposing Betrayal: "Abu Bakr al-Suli recounts, 'One king's secrets were constantly being leaked to his enemies, causing his plans to fail. One day, he lamented to one of his friends, "Some are revealing my secrets, but I do not know who. I fear punishing an innocent person unintentionally."'" "In response, his friend summoned a scribe and had several letters written, each containing false information about a different affair of the kingdom. All of these were fabrications." "Later, he called the official and instructed, 'Deliver one of these to each officer to whom you suspect my state secrets were divulged. However, record which information you

give to whom and admonish them not to disclose it to anyone else!'"
"Shortly afterward, based on the spread of information, the traitors were identified, while the loyal ones who received the real information did not spread it. Thus, the king learned who was leaking his secrets and protected himself from their harm."

Words of Wisdom by Vizier Fakh al-Malik

Against Espionage: "Vizier Fakh al-Malik wrote to someone accused of espionage: 'Even if it is for advice, espionage is an ugly deed. In any case, the harm outweighs the benefit. I do not engage in risky ventures and do not listen to the words of disrespectful individuals. If it were not for my rank, I would have given you a response equivalent to your actions, which would serve as a lesson to others like you. Cease this activity and feel ashamed before the All-knowing (Allah), who observes both good and evil.'"

Muhammed b. Abdulmalik al-Hamadani's Narrative

"In his historical work, Muhammed b. Abdulmalik al-Hamadani recounts how a Kurdish gang conducted robberies in the high mountains, eluding capture due to the rugged terrain. Hearing of this, Caliph Adud al-Dawla summoned a merchant, gave him a mule, and loaded two chests of sweets laced with poison. The sweets looked and smelled delightful. Alongside a sum of money, the Caliph instructed the merchant to present these sweets as a gift to the wife of a provincial governor and travel with a caravan. The merchant walked ahead of the caravan with his mule. The bandits intercepted them on the way, plundered all goods and possessions, leaving everyone stripped naked. They also took the mule and retreated to the mountains. Upon opening the chests, the sweet aroma filled the air, and the sight was mesmerizing. Realizing they couldn't eat it alone, the gang leader called all his men. They devoured the sweets greedily after a long hunger, and as a result, they were all poisoned and perished. The caravan owners retrieved their goods and belongings. I had never heard of such a trap. Adud al-Dawla thus uprooted the rebels and disrupted the troublemakers' reign."

The Merchant's Dilemma and Resolution

Buried Treasure

"A merchant from Horasan prepared to embark on Hajj. Before leaving, he buried an excess of a thousand dinars under a hemp tree in the desert, fearing both the risk of carrying it and the possibility of denial if left in someone's care. Upon returning from Hajj, he couldn't find the money buried under the tree. Distraught, he began to lament and beat himself, telling inquirers that his money had been stolen. Advised to seek Caliph Adud al-Dawla's wisdom, he hesitated, questioning how the Caliph could know the unseen. Persuaded that there was no harm in going, he set off to the Caliph and explained his situation. After pondering for a while, Adud al-Dawla gathered physicians and asked if any of them had treated someone with hemp root recently. One replied affirmatively, mentioning treating someone from the merchant's entourage. When asked, the merchant confirmed he had indeed used it. Asked where he obtained it, he brought the seller who claimed to have extracted it from a spot in the desert. Adding a few more people, the Caliph instructed them to show the location. The seller pointed out the place, and the Horasani merchant exclaimed, 'Here is where I buried my money!' When the Caliph asked him to unearth the money, the man stammered but eventually went and retrieved it."

Gıyas b. Ibrahim reports from al-Medaayini:

"Caliph Abu Ca'fer confronted Ma'an b. Zaaide, who approached him with heavy steps: 'O Ma'an! You have aged!'

'Yes, O Amir of the Faithful! In the path of obedience to you...'

'You appear to me severe and harsh.'

'Against your enemies...'

'It seems there is more to you than meets the eye!'

'For you (to use)...'

'For you (to use) in...'

'Your (endeavors)...'

Caliph Abu Ca'fer then turned to Ma'an b. Zaaide:

'Which is better, my council or your house, O Abdullah?'

'Certainly, your council that rules with justice, O Amir of the Faithful!'

'No, I inquire not about that but about your way of life.'

'Then my house is better.'

'Why?'

'Because I am the owner of my house, whereas here I am the one owned!'

Incident Narrated by Muhammed b. Abdilmalik al-Hemedaani

Muhammed b. Abdilmalik al-Hemedaani recounts:

"One day, Ahmed b. Tolun was sitting on his balcony, having his meal. At one point, he noticed a beggar passing by in tattered clothes. He sent him bread and chicken. Later, his servant reported that the beggar didn't even look at the food. Ahmed b. Tolun doubted this and ordered the beggar to be brought before him. The beggar answered all questions calmly and without hesitation. Ahmed said, 'Take out the letters you carry and tell me who sent you! I have precise information about where you delivered the news.' When the man refused to speak, he ordered a whip to be brought. Upon seeing the whip, the man confessed to carrying messages. Others exclaimed, 'This is sorcery!' Ahmed b. Tolun responded, 'No, it's not sorcery but a fair deduction. I sent him food seeing his distress, offering a meal even the satisfied wouldn't reject. Yet he showed courage in response. Despite his distress, I understood he came for an important task.'"

Ahmed b. Tolun's Judgment

Ahmed b. Tolun observed imams in mosques early in the morning, listening to their recitations. One day, he called a friend and said, 'Go to such and such mosque and give these dinars to the imam.' His friend later recounted:

"I went and sat with the imam. We began conversing, and as the conversation progressed, the imam opened up, explaining that his wife was ill, and he lacked the means to treat her, causing distraction during prayers. I returned and informed Ibn Tolun, who confirmed, 'He speaks the truth. I visited the mosque yesterday and noticed many mistakes in prayer, realizing something was troubling him.'"

Story by Huseyin b. Hasan b. Ahmed b. Yahya al-Waasiki:

My grandfather was the police chief of Baghdad during the caliphate of al-Muktafi Billaah. Once, there were major thefts in the city, and merchants gathered to complain to the caliph. As a result, my grandfather was tasked to catch the thieves or compensate for the losses. He started patrolling alone at night to catch them. One night, while patrolling the outskirts of Baghdad, he entered a dark alley and saw a giant fish skeleton hanging from a house, worth about 120 kilograms. When he asked its value, the fishermen said it was worth a dinar. My grandfather thought about the poverty of the people in that area and how difficult it would be to bring such a large fish there, especially since it led to the desert. To gather information, he knocked on the door of a neighboring house under the pretext of asking for water. An elderly woman opened the door. While drinking water, my grandfather asked her about the situation in the neighborhood. She unknowingly provided him with information. Later, he gathered ten policemen and climbed onto the roofs of nearby houses. He then knocked on the door of the house with the fish skeleton. A servant child opened the door, and inside were five young men who were later taken to the police station and confessed to the thefts. This incident became a source of pride for my grandfather, and he used to recount it often.

Story of Ibn Nisevi's secretary detecting theft:

- Narrator: Two people accused of theft were brought to Ibn Nisevi. Both denied the accusations. Ibn Nisevi asked for a glass of water, intentionally dropped and broke it. One of the accused flinched, while the other remained composed. He told the flinching one to go and the composed one to bring him what they had stolen. When asked how he knew, Ibn Nisevi explained that a thief would remain calm, whereas an innocent person would flinch. The flinching one was innocent, and his reaction helped catch the real thieves.

Legal matter involving a woman's complaint to Caliph Umar:

- Narrator: A woman complained to Caliph Umar about her husband, who was praised as a devout man but neglected her. Umar ordered both the woman and her husband to be brought to him for judgment. After hearing their sides, Umar instructed them to observe a specific regimen of fasting and marital relations, ensuring fairness in the resolution.

Two people were arguing with each other over a sheep with tags on its ears. Each claimed the sheep was theirs. Then someone passed by them. They said to the man, "Judge between us, and we will accept your judgment." The man said, "Then leave the sheep!" He then took the released sheep by the ears and took it away. The other two looked after him and said nothing.

"A man came to Qadi Abu Hazim and said, 'The devil is troubling me, whispering to me that I divorced my wife, causing me to doubt.' The judge asked, 'Did you actually divorce your wife?' The man replied, 'No! I did not divorce her.' The judge then asked, 'Wasn't it you who came to me yesterday and said you had divorced your wife?' The man replied, 'Today is my first time coming to you, and I swear by Allah, I did not divorce my wife in your presence or otherwise.' The judge then advised, 'When the devil comes to you again, swear in the same way to me, and you will find peace.'"

Ibrahim en-Nehaai (r.h.)

Jarir b. Mughir narrates, "When Ibrahim did not want to meet someone, his servant would go out and say, 'Look at the mosque!'"

A'mes narrates:

A man came to Ibrahim and asked, "I spoke about someone. My words reached him. How should I apologize to him?" Ibrahim advised him, "By Allah, surely Allah knows whatever I have said!"

A man approached Abu Hanifa, saying he had buried treasure but couldn't remember where. Abu Hanifa replied, "This isn't a matter of jurisprudence, but I'll give you advice. Go home, pray all night until dawn, and God willing, you'll remember." The man followed his advice and remembered the location of the treasure before the night was over. When he returned the next morning to inform Abu Hanifa, he remarked, "I knew Satan wouldn't leave you alone to pray. You should have spent the rest of the night thanking God!"

Ibn 'ul-Mubaarek

Ibn Humeyde recounts: "A man sneezed near Ibn 'ul-Mubarek and didn't say 'Alhamdulillah.' Ibn 'ul-Mubarek asked him, 'What does one say when sneezing?' When the man replied, 'He says 'Alhamdulillah," Ibn 'ul-Mubarek responded, 'May God have mercy on you.'"

One day, Harun al-Rashid asked Abu Yusuf which of two dishes tasted better. Abu Yusuf replied, 'O Commander of the Faithful! I cannot judge without tasting.' Harun al-Rashid then brought a portion of each dish for him to taste. Abu Yusuf took a bite from each until both were half-eaten. He then turned to the Caliph and remarked, 'O Commander of the Faithful! I have never seen such a strict judge. Whenever I am about to prefer one, the other presents compelling evidence.'

Yezid b. Harun

Yahya b. Said al-Kattaan recounts: "Yezid b. Harun once told me, 'You are heavier than half of a millstone to me.' When I asked why not heavier than the whole, he replied, 'Because a whole millstone rolls by itself, while a half can only be moved with great effort.'"

- Azhar b. Abdulwahhab narrates: "A man came to Ibn Ukayl and asked, 'I immersed myself in the river two or three times for ghusl, but I still feel that the water did not swallow me completely and I am not fully clean. What should I do?' Ibn Ukayl replied, 'In this case, do not pray!' When the man asked, 'How can you say that?' Ibn Ukayl responded, 'Because the Prophet (peace be upon him) said, "The responsibility is lifted from three people: the child until he reaches maturity, the sleeper until he wakes up, and the insane person until he recovers his senses." Anyone who thinks he has not been cleaned after immersing in water two or three times is considered insane.'"

- A jurist advised someone who asked, "When I enter the river to take off my clothes and bathe, should I turn towards the Qibla or another direction?" The jurist replied, "Turn towards where your clothes are."

- Junayd narrates from Sirri (Sakati): "I fell ill in Tarsus, and the Kumas came to visit me, staying longer than necessary. When they were about to leave, they asked me to make a prayer. I raised my hands and prayed, 'O Allah, teach us the manners of visiting the sick!'"

- El-Atibi narrates: "One night in Basra, the wind stopped, and the heat increased. The next day, a Bedouin was asked, 'How was the weather last night?' He replied, 'It seemed to stop just to listen!'"

The Deceptive Youth

Abdulmalik b. Umeyr narrates from Mugire b. Shuba: "In my lifetime, no one has deceived me except a young man from the Beni'l-Hasr b. Ka'b tribe. I asked him about a woman from his tribe. He told me, 'O Amir! She will bring you no good; I saw another man kissing her.' Because of this, I gave up on the woman. However, a few days later, I heard that he had married her himself. When I sent word to remind him of what he had told me, he replied, 'It's true, I saw her father kissing her.' I always regret remembering his deception."

An Intelligent Wife's Solution

In Kufa, there was a woman whose husband was struggling to make ends meet.

One day, the woman said to her husband, "Why don't you go on a journey to seek Allah's blessings and provisions?"

The man traveled to Damascus, worked for a while, and earned three hundred dirhams with which he bought a fine camel.

However, the unruly camel drove him to frustration on the return journey, prompting him to say, "By Allah, if I don't sell you for a dirham when we reach Kufa, my wife will be divorced!"

Later, he regretted his words, but it was too late.

When he got home and explained the situation, his wife tied a cat to the camel's neck and went to the market, shouting, "Who will buy this cat for three hundred dirhams and this camel for one dirham?"

Qualities of an Intelligent Muslim

The first way to achieve intelligence is by building and protecting our iman (faith) through the correct aqeedah (based on Quran, authentic Hadeeth, and the way of the Salaf), good deeds and avoiding sins. Good deeds can boost our iman (faith) and lead to a happier heart. Conversely, sins weaken iman and lead to sadness and despair.

Imam Ibn al-Qayyim beautifully expressed that even if a person finds some fleeting pleasure in sin, it quickly fades, leaving behind only regret and accountability before Allah. Meanwhile, the effort and hardship in performing good deeds may seem difficult at first, but they result in lasting joy and the pleasure of Allah.

Think about Ramadan, for example. During this holy month, we strive through fasting, prayers, and extra acts of worship. Despite the physical challenges, the joy we feel when breaking our fast or completing our prayers is incomparable. This joy continues even after Ramadan ends. Those who engage fully in the worship of Allah often miss Ramadan when it's over because of the spiritual highs they experienced.

The second key is remembrance of Allah (dhikr). Remembering Allah frequently in our daily lives brings a profound sense of peace and happiness. Whether we are traveling, at home, or starting our day, making dhikr keeps our hearts connected to Allah.

Allah says in the Quran that those who remember Him often are among the successful. A true believer's success lies in their constant connection with Allah. This isn't limited to specific prayers or supplications; it's about keeping Allah in mind in all we do.

For example, when we say "SubhanAllah" (Glory be to Allah), we should reflect on the marvels of His creation—the stars, the oceans, the forests. This brings about a deeper appreciation and contentment in our hearts.

The third step is gratitude (shukr). Being thankful for Allah's blessings brings more happiness into our lives. Allah promises in the Quran that if we are grateful, He will give us more.

The Prophet Muhammad (peace be upon him) exemplified this. Despite his guaranteed forgiveness, he performed extensive acts of worship, and when asked why, he replied that he wanted to be a grateful servant.

Being grateful means acknowledging Allah's favors and using them wisely. For example, if Allah blesses you with wealth, give in charity. If you have good health, use it to perform good deeds. Gratitude helps us see how fortunate we are and keeps us from feeling dissatisfied or depressed.

In the past, some misguided individuals, led astray by Shaytan, attempted to merge and morph the teachings of Neoplatonists, Gnostics, and other such philosophies. These people believed that the path to salvation was found solely in inner knowledge. They asserted that one's heart could directly connect with and guide them to the Divine, claiming that their heart alone would lead them to the best ways to discipline themselves and navigate life's challenges. They favored an impractical approach to religion, insisting that one must completely transform oneself, in contrast to Islam's teaching.

Islam advocates for using one's inherent traits, both strengths and weaknesses, and refining them. It does not demand a complete overhaul of one's nature but encourages turning weaknesses into strengths. For instance, a person may have a quality that Shaytan exploits negatively. However, this very trait can be redirected positively. A cowardly person might be naturally shy and apprehensive, which could protect them from engaging in harmful behaviors. This shyness, when redirected, could become a strength, helping them to seclude themselves from evil and avoid temptation. Similarly, someone with courage and audacity could, under Shaytan's influence, become a warrior against the truth.

Shaytan is like a predator, detecting and exploiting both our strengths and vulnerabilities. He uses our strengths against us and our weaknesses to our detriment. Islam, on the other hand, seeks to refine and enhance whatever qualities we possess, without necessitating a complete transformation of our being. A parable illustrates this idea:

Imagine people in a town hearing that a flood is approaching. One group decides to build a massive wall to block the floodwaters. However, as the water rises, it eventually overtakes the wall. A second group decides to reinforce the buildings and structures in the path of the flood. Despite their efforts, the flood's force causes the buildings to collapse. The third group, representing the people of intelligence and understanding, digs canals to channel the water to places where it can be beneficial, providing sustenance and utility to the people.

This parable highlights the idea that, instead of merely trying to suppress our impulses or fortify ourselves against them, we should learn to redirect these natural inclinations for good. We should identify our strengths and weaknesses and use the teachings of Islam to channel these traits in beneficial ways.

Human nature cannot be entirely changed, but it can be redirected to serve a greater purpose. For example, a person who is naturally introverted and enjoys reading might not be suitable for a role that requires them to act as security at a mosque. Similarly, a naturally extroverted and vigilant person might not be the best candidate for deep, scholarly study. Each person should understand and embrace their unique traits, using them to their advantage within the framework of Islam.

Understanding the soul and one's own nature begins with knowing Allah. Some scholars have said, "Whoever does not know their Lord will not know themselves." This knowledge is the foundation for understanding reality. Allah, who created us, knows us best and provides a religion designed to repair and refine our condition. This guidance helps us understand who we are and how to use our traits beneficially, aligning our lives with His wisdom and mercy.

The fourth step is selflessness. Being selfless means putting others' needs before our own and being in their service. This doesn't mean neglecting our own well-being but rather finding ways to help and support others within our capacity.

The Prophet Muhammad (peace be upon him) said that helping a brother in need is more beloved to him than performing a month of i'tikaf (spiritual retreat) in the mosque. Being beneficial to others and bringing joy to them is one of the best deeds we can do.

This selflessness brings us joy and fulfillment, knowing that we are making a positive impact on others' lives.

The fifth step is positivity. Always strive to look at the bright side of things. Being positive and optimistic helps us navigate life's challenges more effectively. The Prophet Muhammad (peace be upon him) loved optimism and always encouraged his followers to maintain a hopeful outlook.

Even in difficult situations, the Prophet would reassure people and remind them of Allah's mercy and blessings. Focusing on the positives helps us stay content and motivated, and it prevents us from falling into despair.

The final step is balance. Balance is crucial in all aspects of life. The Prophet Muhammad (peace be upon him) maintained a balance between worship, family, and community duties.

He advised us to dedicate time to our faith, our families, and ourselves. This balance helps us avoid burnout and keeps us grounded. It's essential to enjoy halal leisure activities, spend time with loved ones, and engage in community service.

Having this balanced approach allows us to fulfill our responsibilities while enjoying life, leading to true happiness and contentment.

A visionary and intelligent Muslim is someone who always plans and strives for self-improvement. They set goals and work diligently towards them with strong determination. Vision, in its essence, means to visualize something, to see something in the future and believe in it deeply. It can be a dream or a change you wish to see in society

The scope of a person's vision can vary. Some may focus on impacting their local community, while others may have a global vision. The larger the vision, the more collaborative effort is required. As one leadership scholar said, a vision achieved alone isn't big enough. It must involve working with others.

Even the prophets had visions and trusted in Allah. Our ultimate vision should be to meet Allah with His pleasure. Alongside this, we can have personal visions that drive us in life, like working for a cause. These smaller goals help us achieve our greater vision of pleasing Allah and entering paradise. Our actions, though part of Allah's plan, are means through which we strive to fulfill our potential and legacy. Allah knows our destiny, but we don't, and we must act to uncover and fulfill it.

Every action we take and every step we plan are part of our testimony before Allah. We all have unique qualities given by Allah. Identifying and nurturing these through planning and determination are key to being visionary Muslims.

A visionary Muslim possesses four main characteristics: planning, determination, self-evaluation, and positivity. They set clear plans, maintain strong resolve, regularly assess their progress, and believe in their cause.

Planning is essential. As the saying goes, 'If you fail to plan, you plan to fail.' The Prophet Muhammad (peace be upon him) exemplified meticulous planning. He aimed for a global impact, striving to have the most followers on the Day of Judgment. This required strategic planning and execution.

A well-planned vision often extends beyond one's lifetime, creating a lasting legacy. Visionary people, like Malcolm X envisioned a future they didn't fully see but set in motion changes that continue today. Similarly, our efforts should aim for lasting impact, even beyond our lifetimes.

Determination is crucial. It drives us to keep going despite challenges. Fear and complacency can hinder our progress. We must believe in our abilities and strive towards our goals. Staying positive and trusting in Allah's guidance are vital.

Self-evaluation helps us stay on track and adjust our course as needed. Regularly reflecting on our progress ensures we are moving towards our goals. Positivity keeps us motivated and resilient. Believing in our cause and its importance propels us forward, even when faced with obstacles.

To become an intelligent Muslim, it's crucial to start by identifying our main responsibilities. For each responsibility, we need to set clear aims and then devise a plan to achieve those aims.

Let's break it down into three steps:

1. List Your Main Responsibilities: Identify the key areas where you hold significant responsibilities. For Muslims, these often include:

o Worship and devotion to Allah.

o Family responsibilities, including relationships with spouses, children, and parents.

o Career or societal roles.

o Positive influence on your community, including Dawah and outreach.

2. Set Specific Aims for Each Responsibility: Define clear, achievable goals for each area. For example, in worship, your aim might be to achieve the pleasure of Allah through consistent and sincere acts of devotion.

3. Create and Implement a Plan: Develop actionable steps to reach your goals. For worship, this could mean setting a schedule for daily prayers, Quran recitation, and secret good deeds known only to Allah.

For family, the aim might be to foster strong, loving relationships and ensure the spiritual and moral upbringing of children. Your plan could include:

• Daily quality time with your spouse and children.

• Regular calls to parents to maintain bonds.

• Leading by example in practicing and teaching Islamic values at home.

In terms of career, your aim could be to excel in your profession while maintaining Islamic ethics. Your plan might involve:

• Pursuing continuous learning and skills development.

• Striving for excellence in your work to benefit society.

• Balancing your professional responsibilities with your spiritual duties.

A common misconception is the idea that being intelligent and productive means doing everything and saying yes to every opportunity.

True productivity involves focusing on what is genuinely beneficial and learning to say no to distractions that do not align with your goals.

It's crucial to recognize your strengths and limitations. Specialize in areas where you can excel and contribute most effectively, and support others in their strengths. Remember, you are human, not a robot. It's okay to have ups and downs, and it's more important to strive for consistent, meaningful progress rather than trying to do everything at once.

Conclusion

Our Prophet, peace and blessings be upon him, said in an authentic hadith reported by Imam Muslim:

"The strong believer is better and more beloved to Allah than the weak believer, but there is good in both. Strive for what benefits you and seek help from Allah, and do not be helpless. If something befalls you, do not say, 'If only I had done such and such,' but say, 'Qadar Allah wa ma sha' fa'al' (It is the decree of Allah, and He does whatever He wills). For saying 'if' opens the door for Shaytan."

1. "The strong believer is better and more beloved to Allah than the weak believer, but there is good in both." This does not refer to physical strength but to the strength of faith (Iman). Not everyone's faith is at the same level; it fluctuates. The stronger one's faith, the more beloved they are to Allah. This is evident in both our actions and interactions with others. Even within ourselves, our faith can vary throughout the year. Our Prophet, peace be upon him, reminds us that the believer with strong faith is more beloved to Allah. This calls us to examine our own faith and strive to strengthen it through our inner and outer deeds. To be an intelligent Muslim reflect on how often you remember Allah, how consistent you are in prayer, and how you avoid sins.

2. Allah's love varies. Allah's love for a person can change over time. For instance, before embracing Islam, the Companions' deeds were not beloved to Allah. But once they embraced Islam and bettered themselves, Allah's love for them increased. This should prompt us to consider our own relationship with Allah and how we can earn His love. To achieve this, we should embody qualities that Allah loves, as mentioned in the Quran: taqwa (consciousness of Allah), patience, and other righteous

traits. Simultaneously, we should avoid characteristics that Allah dislikes, such as extravagance and wrongdoing.

3. "But there is good in both." The hadith emphasizes that even a weak believer possesses goodness. This encourages us not to lose hope, even if we feel our faith is not strong. The Prophet, peace be upon him, teaches us to recognize the good in every believer and to always strive for improvement.

4. "Strive for what benefits you and seek help from Allah." Determination and planning are essential. Whether in religious or worldly matters, aim for what is most beneficial. For example, seek the best education or strive to be a righteous person. After setting your goal, seek Allah's help. This reflects the attitude of the believer who knows that without Allah's support, nothing can be achieved. Therefore, we should make dua (supplication) for Allah's assistance and guidance. This also includes ensuring our actions align with what is halal (permissible).

5. "Do not be helpless." Even if things do not go as planned, do not despair. Do not dwell on "what ifs" or regret past decisions. Accept Allah's decree with contentment. This mindset keeps Shaytan at bay and fosters a positive outlook on life.

6. "It is the decree of Allah, and He does whatever He wills." This part of the hadith emphasizes acceptance of Allah's will. Whatever happens, acknowledge that it is Allah's decree and part of His plan. This instills a sense of peace and submission to Allah's wisdom.

Before starting any endeavor we should ensure that we have the right intentions and that we pray to Allah for guidance. This is crucial preparation before taking action. Brothers and sisters, think about the last major project you undertook. Most of us usually dive in without these necessary preconditions of having a noble goal and correct intentions. Ask yourself, why are you pursuing this? Ensure your intentions are pure; it should benefit both your religious and worldly life, not just one.

Everything beneficial for your religion is also beneficial for your worldly life. However, not everything beneficial for your worldly life is beneficial for your religion. For example, memorizing the Quran or regular prayer will bring blessings in this world too. But aiming solely for material gain may harm your spiritual well-being.

So, before starting anything new, ensure two things: have the right goal and the right intentions. Then, make dua to Allah. This hadith outlines three steps.

Firstly, have the right mindset and make dua.

Secondly, there's no substitute for hard work. It's about effort—tilling before planting, studying before exams, or training before becoming a professional.

Thirdly, after having the right mindset and praying, work diligently. Don't just sit back thinking Allah will provide without your effort. Success doesn't come without toil—be it in education, business, or any endeavor. Don't be lazy or give up prematurely. This approach shows our religion combines spiritual goals with practical effort. We need both the right intentions and dedicated hard work for success.

These three steps are crucial for success. First, have sincere intentions and determination. Second, make dua to Allah. Third, put in the necessary effort—there's no substitute for hard work. Without these, you won't achieve your goals properly.

Suppose you followed these steps and still faced failure or an unexpected outcome. Remember what the Prophet said: "If something happens to you, don't say 'if only,' but instead say 'Allah decreed and what He willed has happened.'" Ultimately, success isn't just achieving your goals; it's pleasing Allah. Trust His plan even if it differs from yours.

Sometimes, despite doing everything right—having good intentions, making dua, and working hard—the outcome may not align with our plans. Allah's plan is often different and better for us. Don't dwell on what could have been done differently. Trust that Allah's plan is better, even if it's not immediately clear.

This hadith provides profound psychological insights. It guides our mindset before, during, and after any action. It encourages optimism and proactive effort, alongside trusting Allah's plan. Our religion doesn't advocate passivity but proactive faith, combining spiritual devotion with practical endeavor.

When faced with major decisions, practice Salatul Istikhara. It's a neglected but powerful blessing. This prayer seeks Allah's guidance before any significant decision. Our Prophet recommended it for any major matter, seeking Allah's choice between options. It's a simple two-unit prayer, followed by a specific dua, asking for guidance. Trusting in Allah, you proceed with the decision, knowing His answer will unfold—either through eased paths or obstacles.

Avoid superstitious beliefs about Istikhara, like interpreting dreams or signs. The true response is in the ease or difficulty experienced afterward, guided by the prayer's dua. Istikhara isn't a magic solution but a means to align our choices with Allah's will. Trust His decision, even if it defies our immediate desires.

The Messenger of Allah (peace be upon him) said: 'Indeed, health and free time are two blessings from Allah Almighty. Many people are deceived regarding them.'

The Messenger of Allah (peace be upon him) said: 'The intelligent person is one who judges himself and works for what comes after death, while the weak person is one who follows his own desires and indulges in wishful thinking about Allah Almighty.'

From Abu Hurairah that the Messenger of Allah (peace be upon him) said: 'Hasten to perform good deeds before seven events: Are you waiting for poverty that makes you forgetful, or wealth that corrupts, or illness that harms, or senility that makes you mentally unstable, or death that comes suddenly, or the Antichrist (Dajjal) who is the worst troublemaker, or the Hour (Day of Judgment) which is more calamitous and bitter.'"

This Hadith emphasizes the importance of proactive righteousness and preparedness for the Hereafter, warning against the distractions and pitfalls of worldly desires and procrastination in matters of faith and good deeds.

Key Takeaways to become an intelligent Muslim:

1. Identify Responsibilities: Focus on key areas like worship, family, career, and community.

2. Set Clear Goals: Define specific aims for each responsibility.

3. Develop a Plan: Create actionable steps to achieve these goals.

4. Avoid Sin: Stay away from actions that remove blessings and productivity.

5. Stay Focused: Specialize in what you're good at and learn to say no to distractions.

6. Embrace Humanity: Recognize your limitations and strive for consistent progress.

So, seize the day and don't waste your time if you truly want to be an intelligent Muslim.

Oh people, be mindful of your Lord and fear Allah, through whom you ask one another, and the wombs (kinship). Indeed, Allah is ever an Observer over you. Oh, you who believe, fear Allah and speak straightforwardly. He will correct your deeds and forgive your sins. And whoever obeys Allah and His Messenger has certainly attained a great success.

www.ingramcontent.com/pod-product-compliance
Lightning Source LLC
Chambersburg PA
CBHW051905130726
47987CB00002B/987